Legal Entities and Relationships

Arlene Blatt

Judith M. Wolf

2014
Emond Montgomery Publications
Toronto, Canada

Emond Montgomery Publications Limited
60 Shaftesbury Avenue
Toronto ON M4T 1A3
http://www.emp.ca/highered

Printed in Canada.
Reprinted November 2014.

We acknowledge the financial support of the Government of Canada through the Canada Book Fund for our publishing activities.

Sample Form 1 under the *Business Corporations Act*, reproduced on pages 27-32, was prepared by Emond Montgomery Publications for information purposes only. Blank copies of the Articles of Incorporation—Form 1—*Business Corporations Act* may be obtained from ServiceOntario at http://www.forms.ssb.gov.on.ca/mbs/ssb/forms/ssbforms.nsf/FormDetail ?openform&ENV=WWE&NO=007-07116. Form © Queen's Printer for Ontario, 2008. Reproduced with permission.

Emond Montgomery Publications has no responsibility for the persistence or accuracy of URLs for external or third-party Internet websites referred to in this publication, and does not guarantee that any content on such websites is, or will remain, accurate or appropriate.

Publisher, Higher Education: Mike Thompson
Director, editorial and production: Jim Lyons
Production editor: Andrew Gordon
Copy editor: Jamie Bush
Permissions editor: Nancy Ennis
Proofreaders: David Handelsman, Daniel Polowin
Indexer: Paula Pike
Cover and text designer and typesetter: Tara Wells
Cover image: © Blue Jean Images/Corbis

ISBN 978-1-55239-574-5

The Library and Archives Canada CIP record for this book is available from the publisher on request.

To my late father, Leonard Blatt, who quietly inspired me, always.
A.B.

To the three pillars in my life: my parents, for your incredible love,
support and guidance; and Erin, for being you.
J.M.W.

Contents

PART III

ESTATE PLANNING AND ADMINISTRATION

Preface

This book provides a general overview of various legal entities and relationships, including the basic concepts and terminology of business law, property law, mortgages, wills and estates, and powers of attorney. Although these areas of law are outside of the permitted scope of practice for paralegals and court clerks, they are often the subject matter of actions and proceedings in Ontario courts and tribunals. Therefore, it is very helpful for paralegals and court clerks to have an understanding of these legal topics.

Small Claims Court is a significant area of practice for paralegals. Pursuant to subsection 6(2) of the Law Society's By-Law 4, licensed paralegals who are representing clients in Small Claims Court are authorized to

- give a party advice on his, her, or its legal interests, rights, or responsibilities with respect to a proceeding or the subject matter of a proceeding;
- select, draft, complete or revise, or assist in the selection, drafting, completion or revision of, a document for use in a proceeding;
- negotiate a party's legal interests, rights, or responsibilities with respect to a proceeding or the subject matter of a proceeding; and
- select, draft, complete or revise, or assist in the selection, drafting, completion or revision of, a document that affects a party's legal interests, rights, or responsibilities with respect to a proceeding or the subject matter of a proceeding.

Furthermore, rule 3.01(1) of the Paralegal Rules of Conduct requires that a paralegal perform legal services to the standard of a competent paralegal. Rule 3.01(4) defines a competent paralegal as one who knows, among other things, the "general legal principles and procedures and the substantive law and procedures for the legal services that the paralegal provides."

Competency has become more of an issue since the monetary jurisdiction of the Small Claims Court increased from $10,000 to $25,000. Not only have the number and complexity of cases heard in this court increased as a consequence, but there has also been an increase in the areas of substantive law being dealt with in Small Claims Court actions. More than ever before, paralegals must have a general knowledge and understanding of legal concepts and terms that might be relevant to a Small Claims Court proceeding. This will help them meet the competency requirements set out in the Paralegal Rules of Conduct.

Let's look at some examples. Real estate law is not a permitted area of practice for paralegals. However, if representing a party who is suing for damages resulting from the sale of a home, a paralegal needs to understand basic real estate concepts. Similarly, if the party being sued is a business entity, the paralegal will also need a general knowledge of business law concepts and terms so that he or she can competently advise his or her client about business-related matters. The same applies in the area of estates law. Even though paralegals are not permitted to draft wills or provide legal services in this area, a paralegal may be representing a client who wants to sue the estate of a deceased person. A paralegal may also be acting on a matter in which one or more of the litigants are represented by a power of attorney. This means that an understanding of wills and estates is another requirement for a competent licensed paralegal. As you can see from these examples, licensed paralegals must understand the areas of business law, property law, and estates law, even though they are not authorized to provide legal services in these areas.

This book will help paralegals and court clerks understand the general legal principles and substantive law governing these areas.

We want to acknowledge Linda Pasternak, Program Coordinator of Seneca College's Paralegal and Court and Tribunal Administration diploma programs, for recommending that we write this book.

We also want to thank Leah Daniels, Joan Emmans, Jordan Fenton, JoAnn Kurtz, Elise Pulver, Steven Pulver, Evelyn Schusheim, and Larry Track. We appreciate the feedback and clarification they provided.

PART I

Business Organizations

Chapters 1, 2, and 3 discuss three different methods of carrying on a business in Ontario—sole proprietorships, partnerships, and corporations. Anyone looking to start a new business should consider the advantages and disadvantages of each type of business organization before deciding which one best suits his or her needs.

Sole Proprietorships

1

LEARNING OUTCOMES

After reading this chapter, you should be able to:

- Understand how sole proprietorships are created
- Understand how a business operating as a sole proprietorship is controlled
- Know when the name of a sole proprietorship must be registered
- Understand the advantages and disadvantages of sole proprietorships

Introduction

sole proprietorship
a business that is owned and operated by one person

sole proprietor
the owner of a sole proprietorship

unincorporated business
a business that has not been incorporated

legal entity
an individual or business that is responsible for its actions and has the right to enter into contracts, assume and enforce obligations, and sue or be sued

A **sole proprietorship** consists of only one person, known as the **sole proprietor**, who runs the business by him- or herself. A sole proprietorship is an **unincorporated business** and is the simplest, fastest, and least expensive way to set up a new business. Many small business owners who want to keep their costs down will operate their business as a sole proprietorship, with few or no employees. A sole proprietorship is not considered a **legal entity** separate from its owner. In other words, the law treats the sole proprietor and the sole proprietorship as one entity; there is no distinction between the sole proprietor and his/her business. For example, assume that Jake Buddison is the sole proprietor of a small business. Even if Jake hires employees, the business will still be considered a sole proprietorship, as long as Jake is the sole owner. It should be noted that if a sole proprietor has any employees, the sole proprietor must abide by any applicable laws governing employer–employee relationships, such as the *Employment Standards Act* and the *Human Rights Code*, as in any employment situation.

Name of a Sole Proprietorship

A sole proprietor can carry on business either using his or her own name or using a business name. For example, Bryce Aleem may want to call the handyman business he is starting "Bryce Aleem, Handyman." Alternatively, a sole proprietor can use a business name. Bryce Aleem may not want to use his own full name for the business. He may want to call it "Helping Hands" or "Bryce's Helping Hands." Regardless of the name Bryce chooses, his business will be a sole proprietorship and he will be the sole proprietor.

If a sole proprietor uses a business name that does not include his or her own full name, then he or she must register the name with the Ministry of Government Services. This is required pursuant to s. 2(2) of Ontario's *Business Names Act*,[1] which states the following:

> No individual shall carry on business or identify his or her business to the public under a name other than his or her own name unless the name is registered by that individual.

creditor
a party to whom money is owed

The purpose of this requirement is to ensure that anyone dealing with the sole proprietorship can determine who is responsible for the business. For example, someone who hires Bryce's Helping Hands to renovate a kitchen may, if a problem arises with the renovation, want to discuss it with the owner of the company. Or maybe Bryce's Helping Hands has not paid its bills, and a **creditor** is trying to collect money from the business. In either situation, the person dealing with the business has a right to know the identity of the individual responsible for it. Although the name Bryce's Helping Hands includes the owner's first name, it does not indicate that Bryce Aleem

---

1 RSO 1990, c. B.17.

is the sole proprietor. Therefore, the name Bryce's Helping Hands must be registered. With the name registered, a person who needs to identify the sole proprietor can do so by searching the business name. A search would reveal Bryce Aleem's full legal name and address.

Anyone can search a business name. You can do this either in person, at the Companies and Personal Property Security Branch of the Ministry of Government Services, or online using the Business link provided on the ServiceOntario website, at www.ontario.ca/welcome-serviceontario.

Once a business name is registered, it remains valid for five years, at which point it must be renewed. If a business name is not registered, the searcher can obtain a certificate of non-registration, which confirms that the name is not being used, so the proprietor can use it. It is an offence under the *Business Names Act* to carry on business using a name (other than the sole proprietor's own name) that has not been registered.

A sole proprietor can use any name he or she wants, subject to the limitations set out in the *Business Names Act* and in the regulation respecting names made under that Act.[2] Section 4(3) of the *Business Names Act* provides the following:

> Only letters from the Roman alphabet, Arabic numerals or a combination of letters from the Roman alphabet and Arabic numerals together with punctuation marks and such other marks as are prescribed may form part of a registered name.

O. Reg. 122/91 (Restrictions Respecting Names) sets out the requirements, prohibitions, and restrictions for a valid business name. For example, the regulation requires that the first character of the name must be a letter or a number. It also prohibits registration of a name that is made up of only (or mostly) punctuation or other marks, or that uses any words or expressions that are obscene or contrary to public policy.

When choosing a business name, it is a good idea, although not mandatory, to conduct a **NUANS (Newly Upgraded Automated Name Search)** to see whether or not that name, or a very similar name, already exists as a business name or **trademark**. While it is permissible to register a name that is already being used, it is not advisable to do so. The original name holder might have a cause of action for damages if he or she can prove that another person's use of the same or a similar name resulted in loss to him or her of business and/or reputation.

As noted above, if the full name of the sole proprietor is included in the name of the sole proprietorship, then the name does not have to be registered. In this instance, the identity of the sole proprietor is obvious from the name of the sole proprietorship.

NUANS (Newly Upgraded Automated Name Search)
a computerized search that is conducted to find existing business names and trademarks

trademark
a word(s), design, slogan, symbol, logo, or any other mark (or a combination of these) that identifies and distinguishes a person's goods or services from those of all others

Control of a Sole Proprietorship

Because a sole proprietorship is not considered to be a legal entity separate from its owner, the law does not distinguish between the sole proprietor and his or her business. The sole proprietor is entitled to 100 percent of the profits of the sole

2 O. Reg. 122/91, Restrictions Respecting Names, under the *Business Names Act*.

goodwill
the intangible component of the value of a business, such as the business's reputation

proprietorship and is 100 percent responsible for the debts and liabilities of the business. For example, Bryce Aleem, as the sole proprietor of Bryce's Helping Hands, owns the assets, profits, and **goodwill** of Bryce's Helping Hands, but is also personally responsible for the business's debts, taxes, and lease payments, as well as for any other obligations or liabilities the business may incur.

Bryce would also be liable for any actions brought against Bryce's Helping Hands, such as an action for damages resulting from an improperly completed job. A lawsuit against a sole proprietorship may use either the sole proprietor's name alone, or the sole proprietor's name followed by the business name, or the business name alone. For example, if a customer started a claim against Bryce's Helping Hands, the defendant would be named as either

- Bryce Aleem,
- Bryce Aleem carrying on business (cob) or operating as (o/a) Bryce's Helping Hands, or
- Bryce's Helping Hands.

Regardless of what name the plaintiff uses, the judgment would be enforceable against Bryce Aleem. It is always easier to enforce a judgment when the action uses the owner's full name. In other words, if the sole proprietor's name is different from the name of the sole proprietorship (that is, the business), a person starting an action against the business should use both names.

Someone who obtains a judgment against a sole proprietorship can enforce it by going after both the personal and business assets of the sole proprietor. Income earned by a sole proprietorship is treated as income of the sole proprietor. For example, income earned by Bryce's Helping Hands will be treated as Bryce's income, and he will have to pay taxes on this business income at the same rate as his personal income tax rate.

Advantages of a Sole Proprietorship

The main advantage of a sole proprietorship is that it is an easy and inexpensive way to start and to run a business. Other than the requirement described above—that is, the requirement to register the name of the sole proprietorship if it is different from the owner's name—there are no legal formalities involved in setting up and operating this form of business organization. Establishing a sole proprietorship using the business owner's legal name can be as easy as printing up business cards and letterhead and starting the business. Other advantages of a sole proprietorship include the following:

- There is very little regulation from the government.
- The sole proprietor has complete control of the business and can make all decisions him/herself.
- All profits belong to the sole proprietor; they do not have to be shared with anyone.
- A sole proprietor files only one income tax return and can therefore deduct any business losses or expenses from his/her personal income.

The sole proprietor's position with respect to taxes can be a significant advantage if the business suffers a financial loss. For example, assume that Bryce Aleem has a total income of $100,000 from all sources (including non-business income, such as dividends and interest) and has business losses of $25,000. As a sole proprietor, Bryce can deduct these losses and thereby reduce his taxable income from $100,000 to $75,000.

Disadvantages of a Sole Proprietorship

The main disadvantage of a sole proprietorship is that there is unlimited liability. In other words, the sole proprietor is personally liable for all the debts and obligations of the business. This is because the law does not treat the sole proprietor and the sole proprietorship as separate legal entities. For example, assume that while installing a counter in a client's kitchen, Bryce or one of Bryce's Helping Hands' employees accidentally damages the hardwood floors. In this situation, Bryce will be personally liable for the damage caused. This means that if the business cannot afford to pay for the damage, the homeowner can go after Bryce's personal assets, such as his bank account, his equipment, his house, or his car. One way that a sole proprietor can limit his or her **personal liability** is by obtaining insurance to cover potential losses.

personal liability
a business owner's personal responsibility for the debts and obligations of the business

Other disadvantages of a sole proprietorship include the following:

- It may be difficult for a sole proprietor to raise **capital** on his/her own.
- The business may be jeopardized if the sole proprietor becomes ill and there is no one else to run the business.
- The sole proprietor may be taxed at a higher personal tax rate if the business is profitable.
- A sole proprietor is not considered an employee and will not therefore be entitled to employee benefits such as employment insurance, vacation pay, or salary.
- The business ends if the sole proprietor dies.

capital
the financial investment contributed to a business

KEY TERMS

capital, 7
creditor, 4
goodwill, 6
legal entity, 4

NUANS (Newly Upgraded Automated Name Search), 5
personal liability, 7
sole proprietor, 4

sole proprietorship, 4
trademark, 5
unincorporated business, 4

REVIEW QUESTIONS

1. Does the law treat a sole proprietorship and its sole proprietor as one legal entity?   *Yes*

2. Can a sole proprietor include his/her full name as part of the business name?   *Yes*

3. Nyla runs a small business and hires three employees to assist her. Is Nyla a sole proprietor?   *Yes*

4. Roger Rovinka wants to call his new business "Roger's Racquets and Sports." Does Roger have to register this name? Explain your answer.   *Yes cause his A have to have full name*

5. How can someone determine the registered business name of a sole proprietorship?   *Ministry*

6. Danny Trumper is starting a new dry-cleaning business and is considering using one of the following names:

   - ****#1Dry Clean!!!!

   - Danny's Dry Cleaning

   - Dan's Damn-Good Dry Cleaning

   For each of the three names set out above, state whether or not the name is a valid and registrable name for Danny's business.

7. State two advantages and two disadvantages of a sole proprietorship.

Partnerships

2

LEARNING OUTCOMES

After reading this chapter, you should be able to:

- Explain how partnerships are created, named, and governed in Ontario

- Understand the three different types of partnerships with respect to the relationship between partners, the relationship between the partnership and third parties, and partners' liability

- Understand partnership agreements

- Describe how a partnership dissolves

- Explain the advantages and disadvantages of partnerships

Introduction

A partnership consists of two or more people who carry on business together, with a view to making a profit. Someone who doesn't want to be a sole owner and operator of a business might prefer this type of business organization.

In Ontario, partnerships are governed by the *Partnerships Act*.[1] This statute sets out the rules regarding the relationship between the partnership and third parties, as well as the relationship between the partners themselves. Section 2 defines "partnership" as

> the relation that subsists between persons carrying on a business in common with a view to profit, but the relation between the members of a company or association that is incorporated by or under the authority of any special or general Act in force in Ontario or elsewhere, or registered as a corporation under any such Act, is not a partnership within the meaning of this Act.

As this definition indicates, the individuals working within a corporation or association are not in a partnership. However, a corporation itself may be a partner within a partnership.

People can establish a partnership simply by agreeing to work together and then by carrying on a business together, with the intention of making a profit. According to the law, people may create a partnership without entering into a contract. The *Partnerships Act* sets out specific rules for determining whether or not a partnership in fact exists.[2] The main criterion concerns whether the people involved are actually *carrying on a business* together, and not working together for some other purpose. For example, if Rob, Hassan, and Rachel—three musicians—play together one night in a one-off performance, they are not carrying on a business together and their working association does not constitute a partnership. However, if they perform together on a regular basis and share the profits from their concerts, then they will be carrying on a business—the business of performing live music—and a partnership will be formed.

A partnership is not considered to be a legal entity separate from its owners. As with sole proprietorships, the law makes no distinction between the partnership and its members (that is, the partners). In other words, each partner is acting as an agent of the partnership and the other partners when carrying on business related to the partnership. Each partner is responsible, together with the other partners, for the debts and obligations of the partnership.

This means that any income earned by the partnership is treated as income of the partners. Unless there is a **partnership agreement** that states otherwise, partners will share the profits of the partnership equally, and be equally responsible for the losses incurred by the partnership.

partnership agreement
an agreement between partners that defines the terms of their relationship

---

1   RSO 1990, c. P.5.

2   Ibid., s. 3.

Furthermore, because the partnership is not a separate legal entity, each partner will pay tax at his or her own personal tax rate and can deduct any losses incurred through the partnership from his or her own personal income.

Types of Partnerships

There are three types of partnerships in Ontario—the general partnership, the limited partnership, and the limited liability partnership (LLP). These three types differ with respect to the degree of involvement of the partners and the degree of liability one partner bears for the actions of the others.

General Partnership

General partnerships are the most common type. All partners in this kind of partnership have the same degree of power and liability for all partnership-related activities. The *Partnerships Act* governs both the relationship between the partners themselves and the relationship between partners and third parties. A partnership agreement (discussed below) may influence the relationship between the individual partners, but it cannot alter the rights of third parties who conduct business with the partnership. Under the rules set out in the *Partnerships Act*, each partner

- is an agent of the partnership and of the other partners,
- will legally bind the partnership and the other partners while carrying on the business of the partnership,
- is entitled to an equal share of the capital and profits of the business,
- must contribute equally to the losses of the business,
- may take part in the management of the partnership business,
- is personally liable for all debts and obligations of the partnership business, and
- is personally liable for any actions brought against the partnership, or for any actions against another partner who was acting on behalf of the partnership.

Let's look at how these rules might apply to members of a partnership. Assume that Keith, Adam, and Lazaro are partners in a talent agency. If the partnership has expenses that the partnership itself cannot afford to pay, then Keith, Adam, and Lazaro will each be required to pay these expenses out of his personal assets. And, if the talent agency borrows money from the bank, then each of Keith, Adam, and Lazaro is liable for the full amount of the loan. In other words, the bank can sue any one of them for the full amount. The three partners have what is called **joint liability**. Joint liability means that each partner is liable for the full amount of a debt.

Also, if Lazaro carelessly injures someone while carrying out partnership business, not just he but Keith and Adam, too, will be responsible for those injuries. And suppose Keith hires Roger, a musician, to perform at an event, and Keith and Roger enter into a written contract. Even though Adam and Lazaro are not parties to the contract and know nothing about it, they will be bound by its terms and conditions.

joint liability
each partner is fully liable for the full amount of the partnership's debts or of claims against the partnership

Now let's assume Keith breaches the terms of the contract and Roger sues him for damages in the amount of $100,000. Let's also assume that Roger wins and the court orders Keith to pay $100,000. If Keith pays this amount, he then has the right to go after Adam and Lazaro for their respective shares of the $100,000. If, on the other hand, Keith is not able to pay the $100,000, Roger can sue Adam and/or Lazaro and attempt to collect from them. In this situation, Adam or Lazaro, as applicable, can then go after Keith for his proportionate share of the damages.

joint and several liability
state in which (1) each partner is fully liable for the full amount of a creditor's claim or debt, and (2) the partner who pays the full amount can claim against the other partner(s) for the other's share of the claim or debt

The partners in a general partnership are said to have **joint and several liability** for the wrongdoing of any partner acting in the ordinary course of the partnership's business. *Joint and several liability* means that each partner is responsible for the full amount of the loss, as is the case with joint liability. It also means that the partner who pays the full amount of the loss can go after the other partners for their share of the liability.

Partners cannot contract out of their personal liability to third parties. This means that even if there is a partnership agreement (discussed in more detail below) that effectively limits or reduces one partner's liability to third parties for any losses, this provision will not ultimately be enforceable against a third party. Suppose that, in the above example, Keith, Adam, and Lazaro have a partnership agreement which states that Lazaro is responsible for only 10 percent of losses. If Roger can't collect his money from Keith or Adam, Lazaro may have to pay the full amount of the losses, despite the agreement to the contrary. The partnership agreement will give Lazaro the right to recover his money from Keith and Adam, but that right will not affect the right of the third party to collect from Lazaro.

As for decision making, day-to-day business decisions of the partnership may be made by a majority of the partners rather than by all of them. However, all *major* decisions affecting partnership business require the partners' unanimous consent. This means that decisions about such matters as whether to admit a new partner or to pursue a new business venture, or how to invest partnership profits, cannot be made without the consent of all existing partners.

fiduciary duty
the duty of a partner to act honestly, in good faith, and in the best interests of the partnership

Partners have a **fiduciary duty** to the partnership. This means that they have a duty to act honestly and in good faith, and in the best interests of the partnership. Partners must not take inappropriate personal advantage of any information or business opportunity that comes to them through their being members of the partnership.

Limited Partnership

A limited partnership is in many ways similar to a general partnership; it too consists of partners and is formed to carry on the kind of business that a general partnership would carry on. In a limited partnership, however, there are both general partners and limited partners. The law governing limited partnerships, set out in the *Limited Partnerships Act*,[3] requires that a limited partnership must involve at least one general partner and at least one limited partner. Adding a limited partner to the

---

3   RSO 1990, c. L.16.

firm can be a good way for general partners to raise money and retain complete control of the partnership business. It is also an advantage for the limited partner who wants to invest in the business and share in its profits but does not want to get involved in running the business or take greater risk than his or her investment.

There are two main differences between general and limited partners. First, unlike a general partner, a limited partner does not provide any services to the firm or take part in any of the partnership business activities. The only thing a limited partner may contribute to the partnership is money or property.[4] For this reason, limited partners are often considered to be **silent partners** of the business.

The second main difference between a general and a limited partner is that a limited partner's liability toward the partnership and its creditors is limited to his or her financial contribution to the partnership. While general partners have full liability for the debts and obligations of the partnership, a limited partner is liable only for his or her investment—the value of money and property he or she contributed to the partnership.[5] For example, assume that Keith is a limited partner in the partnership he formed with Adam and Lazaro, and invested $25,000. If the partnership is sued for $100,000, Keith's liability for this debt is limited to his initial contribution—$25,000. Adam and Lazaro, however, as general partners, will be responsible for the full amount.

Limited partners can lose their "limited" status if they become closely involved in the business. If they start participating in the management or day-to-day business of the partnership, they will be deemed to be general partners of the partnership, and they will now be fully responsible for the debts and obligations of the partnership, an amount that may exceed the amount of their investment.

A limited partnership, then, must have at least one limited partner, and at least one general partner who runs the business and assumes unlimited liability for the partnership.

> **silent partner**
> someone who contributes money or property to a firm but takes no part in its management or day-to-day business

Limited Liability Partnership

A limited liability partnership is for professionals only, who want to carry on business together but limit their personal liability. A limited liability partnership is one way a professional can protect him- or herself from responsibility for the negligent acts of the other partners. Limited liability partnerships are governed by the *Partnerships Act*. The Act requires that the partners, when forming a limited liability partnership, enter into a written agreement designating their partnership as a limited liability partnership and stating that the *Partnerships Act* governs the agreement.[6] The Act also requires that the firm name contain the words "limited liability partnership" or have the acronym "LLP" at the end, and that the name be registered under the *Business Names Act*.[7]

---

4 Ibid., s. 7(1).

5 Ibid., s. 9.

6 *Partnerships Act*, s. 44.1(1).

7 Ibid., s. 44.3(1).

In a limited liability partnership, each partner is responsible for all the expenses and obligations involved in running the partnership. In addition, each partner is responsible for his/her own negligence, including the negligence of any employees under his/her direct control or supervision. What makes this kind of partnership different from a general partnership is that, with a limited liability partnership, no partner will be liable for any debts or obligations incurred as a result of another partner's negligent acts (or negligent acts of his/her employee) committed while carrying on partnership business. This means that a partner risks personal liability only for his/her own negligence, but not for the negligent acts of any other partner.

For example, assume Marlene, Alex, and Erin are licensed paralegals and form a partnership. While providing legal services for a client, Alex acts negligently and her mistake causes the client to suffer financial loss. In a general partnership, Marlene and Erin would be personally liable for Alex's actions if the partnership assets were insufficient to cover the client's loss. However, in a limited liability partnership, Marlene's and Erin's personal assets would be protected. The protection from liability, however, applies only with respect to claims that arise because of a partner's negligence. Claims for damages for other reasons, such as breach of a contractual obligation, will be dealt with in the same way as for a general partnership. In other words, if Alex—rather than negligently causing a client to suffer financial loss—did not pay rent in accordance with the terms of the partnership's lease agreement, both Marlene and Erin will be personally liable to pay the landlord.

Professionals who form a limited liability partnership are required to maintain professional liability insurance. In the scenario described above, Alex's insurance would cover the client's losses.

Liability in a professional partnership is limited because, even though professionals face extensive liability for their mistakes, they are required to maintain professional liability insurance. Therefore, the clients are protected even though the other partners are not liable.

Partnership Agreement

A partnership agreement is a written agreement that sets out all of the rights and obligations of the partners. Such an agreement is not mandatory, but it is advisable, especially if the partners want to agree to things that are different from what is provided in the governing legislation—that is, the *Partnerships Act* for a general partnership, or the *Limited Partnerships Act* for a limited partnership.

A partnership agreement can deal with many issues, including the following:

- How much capital does each partner have to contribute?
- Who will be responsible for making major decisions?
- How will partners divide the partnership's profits and apportion its losses?
- How will disputes be resolved?
- Can new partners be added?
- What happens if a partner becomes ill or disabled—or dies?

- What happens if a partner wants to leave the partnership? The partnership agreement will usually include a **buy–sell agreement** setting out how the partnership will be split up.

The main advantage of a partnership agreement is that it allows the partners to define many aspects of their business relationship while they are still on good terms and wanting to start a business together. A comprehensive partnership agreement, entered into at the start of the business relationship, sets out how to address all potential problems. Once the relationship breaks down, it will be much more difficult for the partners to act reasonably toward one another.

The only disadvantage of a partnership agreement is the cost of the legal fees required to negotiate and draft it.

If there is a partnership agreement, its terms will prevail over the provisions in the legislation, except with respect to third-party liability. A partnership agreement cannot limit a partner's liability for claims or losses brought by a third party as a result of that partner's negligent actions. In other words, the partnership agreement will only affect the partners who are parties to the partnership agreement, and it will affect them only with respect to each other. The partnership agreement will not affect the rights of third parties.

If an action is brought by a third party against the partnership as a result of one partner's wrongdoing, the third party has the right to attempt to collect his or her loss from each and every partner. Even if the partnership agreement gives a partner a claim for indemnity from the other partner(s), the rights of the third party will not be affected.

Let's look at an example. Assume that Joe, Smally, and Joanne are partners in a business that takes customers on snorkelling excursions and that the three of them have a partnership agreement that provides that Smally is responsible for only 20 percent of any partnership losses. If a customer brings an action against the partnership for injuries caused as a result of a defective snorkel, the customer can claim damages both against the partnership and against Joe, Smally, and Joanne. If Smally ends up having to pay out more than 20 percent of the claim, he will have a claim against Joanne and Joe for the portion that was in excess of the amount he was responsible for under the partnership agreement.

When there is no partnership agreement, the legislation governs all aspects of the partnership.

> **buy–sell agreement**
> an agreement between partners that defines how one partner can buy out the interest of the other partner(s) (also known as a buyout agreement)

Name of a Partnership

When a partnership is created, the partners are known collectively as a "firm," and the name under which they carry on business is called the "firm name" or "partnership name." If the firm name includes the partners' names, it does not have to be registered, unless it is a limited liability partnership. Limited liability partnerships, along with partnerships that use a firm name that does not include the full names of the partners, must register their names under the *Business Names Act*.

As with sole proprietorships, certain words or expressions cannot be included in a firm name. For example, a firm name cannot contain any words that suggest the firm is a corporation, such as the words "Limited," "Corporation," or "Incorporated," or their respective abbreviations "Ltd.," "Corp.," or "Inc." O. Reg. 122/91 (Restrictions Respecting Names), made under the *Business Names Act*, sets out all the requirements, prohibitions, and restrictions for a valid firm name.

In the case of a limited partnership, s. 6(1) of the *Limited Partnerships Act* provides that the surname of a limited partner "shall not appear in the firm name of the limited partnership unless it is also the surname … of one of the general partners." This means that if Jeffrey Matthew is a limited partner, his surname, Matthew, cannot be part of the partnership name unless one of the general partners also has the surname Matthew.

Figure 2.1   Comparison of the Three Types of Partnerships

	General Partnership	**Limited Partnership**	**Limited Liability Partnership**
Description	Two or more people carrying on business together with a view to making a profit	Two or more people carrying on business together with a view to making a profit Partnership must have at least one general partner and one limited partner	Two or more professionals carrying on business together Partners must enter into a written agreement designating the partnership as a limited liability partnership
Name of Partnership	Must be registered if partners' names are not used	Must be registered if partners' names are not used (and name cannot include a limited partner's name)	Must be registered and must end in "limited liability partnership" or "LLP"
Liability of Partners	Unlimited liability: • Joint liability for debts and obligations—each partner is personally liable for debts and obligations of partnership • Joint and several liability for wrongdoing of any partner—each partner can recover from other partners	Unlimited liability for general partners (same as a general partnership) Limited partners' liability is limited to the extent of their investment in the partnership	Unlimited liability, but not for the professional negligence of the other partners

Dissolving a Partnership

In the absence of a partnership agreement that provides otherwise, a partnership dissolves if

- the term fixed for its existence expires,
- the single adventure or undertaking for which it was created terminates,
- a partner gives notice to the other partners of his/her intention to dissolve the partnership,
- a partner dies or becomes **insolvent**,
- it becomes unlawful to continue the business, or
- a court orders the dissolution of the partnership.

insolvent
an entity that is unable to meet its financial obligations as they become due

A court may order dissolution of the partnership in the event that

- a partner becomes mentally incompetent or otherwise incapable of performing his or her part of the partnership agreement,
- a partner has been guilty of conduct that justifies putting an end to the carrying on of the partner's business,
- a partner deliberately breaches the partnership agreement or otherwise acts in a way that makes carrying on the business in partnership with that partner impracticable,
- the partnership business can be carried on only at a loss, or
- under the circumstances, the court considers it just and equitable to dissolve the partnership.

Once a partnership is dissolved, its assets and liabilities will be used to satisfy any partnership debt. Any surplus partnership property will be divided equally among the partners, unless a partnership agreement provides otherwise.

Advantages of a Partnership

Among the advantages of a partnership are the following:

- Partnerships, like sole proprietorships, are fairly easy to establish and are an informal and inexpensive way for two or more people to carry on business together.
- With more than one owner, there may be more capital available to contribute to the partnership.
- Because each partner brings different skills and talents to the firm, a partnership can offer a wide range of services and generate many contacts.
- Finally, the partnership structure offers certain tax advantages in the event that the partnership incurs a loss. Partnerships are treated the same way as

sole proprietorships—the partner's partnership income and personal income are used to determine the partner's taxable income. A partner files only one tax return and can offset business expenses and losses against his/her personal income, thereby reducing overall tax liability.

Disadvantages of a Partnership

Among the disadvantages of the partnership structure are the following:

- The main disadvantage of a partnership is that general partners are personally responsible for the partnership's debts and obligations and for the other partners' wrongful acts or omissions.
- There may be tax disadvantages for a partner if the partnership is profitable, because once his/her partnership income is added to his/her personal income, he/she may end up paying income tax at a higher tax rate.
- There is the potential for disagreements and disputes between the partners.
- An equal sharing of profits may not be the fairest arrangement if partners are not putting equal effort into running or managing the business.
- The partnership can automatically dissolve if one partner becomes ill or dies.

Many of these disadvantages can be avoided, or minimized, by having a partnership agreement.

KEY TERMS

buy–sell agreement, 15
fiduciary duty, 12
insolvent, 17
joint and several liability, 12
joint liability, 11
partnership agreement, 10
silent partner, 13

REVIEW QUESTIONS

1. Myjan, Catherine, and Lucy are employees at the
same business. Are they partners? *No because their employees*

2. Joe and Steve recently started a catering business
together but did not enter into a contract or
agreement with each other. Is their business a
partnership? *Yes*

3. Saraya and Lucia are partners. How will the profits
and losses of their partnership be treated? *Share equally*

4. Brittany and Adam are partners in a fitness club.

   a. They recently received an invoice from a major
   supplier in the amount of $15,000, and the
   partnership does not have enough money to pay
   the full amount. Who is responsible for paying the
   invoice? *both party.*

   b. While training a client, Brittany injures the client,
   and the client starts an action in Small Claims
   Court for damages against Brittany. If the client
   wins the lawsuit, who is responsible for paying
   the damages awarded? *both party.*

5. What is the difference between general partners and
limited partners? *A limited partner is silent while general partner are running the business*

6. Two licensed paralegals want to form a partnership
with an accountant so that they can provide a broad
range of services to their clients. Answer the
following three questions regarding this scenario:

   a. What type of partnership should they enter into?
   Explain your answer. *limited Liability Partnership*

   b. They want to call their partnership "Complete
   Legal and Accounting Services Inc." Is this a valid
   name? Explain your answer. *No you can't Make the Public think your a corporation*

7. State two matters a partnership agreement may deal
with. *profit & a solution*

8. Jose, Joanne, and Tran are partners. Tran recently
died. What will happen to the partnership? *Their Partnership dissolve.*

9. State two advantages and two disadvantages of a
partnership.

Corporations

3

LEARNING OUTCOMES

After reading this chapter, you should be able to:

- Understand the different types of corporations
- Explain how to incorporate a business
- Understand the concept of limited liability
- Explain the rules and restrictions governing a corporation's name, and identify the elements of a valid name
- Identify the people involved in a corporation, and understand their roles within the corporation
- Understand the various corporate documents
- Understand how to dissolve a corporation
- Explain the advantages and disadvantages of corporations

Introduction

A corporation, also known as a "limited company" or simply a "company," is the most common type of business organization. Unlike sole proprietorships and partnerships, a corporation is a legal entity that is separate from its owners. In other words, the law treats the business owner as one entity and the business itself as a different entity. If, for example, Jake Buddison incorporates a business called Buddison Fitness, two separate entities will now exist—Jake Buddison, and Buddison Fitness.

The owners of a corporation are called the **shareholders**. They receive a share in any profits the corporation makes. They receive these profits through the payment of a sum of money known as a **dividend**. (These concepts are discussed in more detail later in this chapter.)

A corporation is created when one or more individuals **incorporate** a business. (The incorporation process is discussed below.) The law that governs incorporation in Ontario defines an "individual" to mean a natural person only.[1] The definition specifically excludes partnerships, unincorporated associations, trusts, and natural persons who are acting as trustees, executors, administrators, or other legal representatives. What this means is that only a natural person can start a corporation.

Corporations are created under the authority of a statute. In Ontario, the statute is the *Business Corporations Act*;[2] in Canada, the statute is the *Canada Business Corporations Act*.[3] A corporation can be incorporated either provincially or federally. (The differences will be discussed later in this chapter.) Unless we state otherwise, the focus in this chapter will be on businesses incorporated in Ontario.

Because a corporation is a legal entity separate from its owners, it has many of the same rights and responsibilities that a natural person has. For example, a corporation can own property, enter into contracts, borrow and lend money, pay taxes, and sue or be sued. The most important feature of a corporation is **limited liability**. This means that the shareholders, directors, and officers of a corporation (positions discussed below) have no personal liability for the debts, obligations, or acts of the corporation. Their liability is limited to their investment in the company. This concept of limited liability is what makes a corporation—for a business owner who wants to protect his or her own personal assets—preferable to any of the other types of business organizations.

For example, assume Bryce Aleem incorporates his handyman business and calls it Helping Hands Inc. If someone sues Helping Hands Inc. for damages arising from faulty work, Helping Hands Inc. will be liable to pay for the loss to the extent that it has sufficient assets. If it does not have sufficient assets to pay for the full amount of the loss, Bryce has no personal liability for this loss. The **plaintiff** can sue only Helping Hands Inc., the incorporated business, and not Bryce personally. Because Bryce incorporated Helping Hands Inc., he has limited liability and is not therefore responsible for the company's financial obligations.

---

shareholder
a corporation or an individual that owns shares in a company

dividend
a payment made to shareholders, which represents a portion of a corporation's profits

incorporate
the process of creating a corporation

limited liability
liability that is limited by law or by agreement; in the case of a corporation, it refers to the lack of personal liability, on the part of shareholders, directors, and officers, for the acts of the corporation

plaintiff
the party that initiates a lawsuit

---

1 *Business Corporations Act*, RSO 1990, c. B.16, s. 1.

2 Ibid.

3 RSC 1985, c. C-44.

It should be noted that there are times when a corporation will not be treated as a separate entity from its shareholders, directors, and officers. When a corporation engages in any type of fraud or other wrongful acts, or is a **sham**, the court may disregard the corporation's legally separate existence and make the directors, officers, and/or shareholders personally responsible for the corporation's actions. This is called **piercing the corporate veil**, and it means that the court will disregard the legal distinction between the corporation and the people behind the corporation. For example, if Bryce Aleem borrows money from the bank on behalf of Helping Hands Inc., but uses the money for himself and then goes ahead and dissolves Helping Hands Inc., the court will likely pierce the corporate veil and find Bryce personally responsible for the money. In this case, it is obvious that the company is a sham; Bryce Aleem created the corporation only as a means of borrowing money that he had no intention of paying back.

Historical Development

The concept of treating a corporation as an entity that is separate from its owners was first established by the 1897 House of Lords decision in the case of *Salomon v. Salomon & Co.*, [1897] AC 22. Aron Salomon was a shoe manufacturer who had run his business for many years as a sole proprietorship before deciding to incorporate. He made each member of his family, including himself, a shareholder. In order to raise money for the business, he personally lent money to the business and secured his money with assets from the corporation. The day-to-day running of the business did not change after he incorporated, and Mr. Salomon continued to take care of the business on his own, as he did when he was a sole proprietor. When the business fell on hard times, the company could not pay its debts in full. As a secured creditor, Mr. Salomon claimed his share of the assets of the corporation together with the other creditors. The other creditors objected, however, saying that Mr. Salomon and the business were one and the same entity and that he should therefore not be entitled to a share of the assets. The court held that the corporation was a separate legal entity from Mr. Salomon and that he was therefore entitled to be paid as a secured creditor.

Types of Corporations

There are three main types of corporations:

1. not-for-profit corporations,
2. professional corporations, and
3. business corporations.

Not-for-profit corporations, unlike the other types of corporations, are not created with the intention of personal financial gain. This type of corporation is created for purposes—for example, charitable, educational, or religious purposes—other than making money for the benefit of the shareholders. The owners, or shareholders, do not own any shares and do not receive any profits from the corporation. Any profits

sham
something that is not what it purports to be (that is, false, not genuine)

piercing the corporate veil (or lifting the corporate veil)
process whereby a court, under certain circumstances— for example, where the corporation has engaged in fraud or other wrongful acts— disregards the corporation's legally separate existence and makes the directors, officers, and/or shareholders personally responsible for the corporation's actions

not-for-profit corporation
a corporation that is created for purposes—for example, charitable, educational, or religious purposes—other than making money for the benefit of the shareholders

or income that a not-for-profit corporation earns are held in trust and are used only to further the goals of the corporation's business; they are not paid out to shareholders. Like other corporations, not-for-profit corporations may be incorporated either provincially or federally.

Professional corporations are corporations made up exclusively of professionals who want to practise together and to use this type of business organization in doing so. The law permits professionals to form a professional corporation as long as the corporation holds a valid certificate of authorization, issued in accordance with the law that governs the profession. For example, take a group of lawyers and licensed paralegals who want to practise law and provide legal services through a professional corporation. They must obtain a certificate of authorization from their governing body, the Law Society of Upper Canada, before practising as a professional corporation.[4]

Business corporations are corporations created for the sole purpose of running a business with a view to profit. They are the most common type of corporation, and for the rest of this chapter, we will be focusing on business corporations alone.

Business corporations can be **private corporations** or **public corporations**. A private corporation is a business corporation that is typically owned by a relatively small number of shareholders and that does not offer its shares to the general public. A public corporation has many shareholders, and the corporation offers its shares, which are traded on the **stock market**, to the general public. Helping Hands Inc. is an example of a private corporation.

The Process of Incorporation

The process of incorporating a business has many formal requirements and is far more complicated than the process of creating either a sole proprietorship or a partnership.

Name of Corporation

The legal name of a corporation can be an actual name. Alternatively, it can be a number that is assigned to the corporation at the time of incorporation, followed by the word "Ontario" and then ending with "Limited," "Incorporated," or "Corporation," or their abbreviations ("Ltd.," "Inc.," or "Corp."). When the name of a company is the assigned number, such as 473737 Ontario Limited, the company is called a **numbered company**.

An **incorporator** will choose to use a number for the name of the company when an actual name is not necessary and the incorporator wants to save the time and expense associated with conducting a name search and thereby speed up the incorporation process. For example, assume Bryce Aleem decides not to use a name for his handyman business and is assigned number 467262 when he incorporates the company. The name of his numbered company will be, for example, 467262 Ontario Limited (or "Ltd.," "Incorporated," or "Inc."). Sometimes, lawyers will incorporate numbered companies just to have them ready for a client who needs a company

private corporation
a small corporation with few shareholders that does not offer its shares to the public

public corporation
a corporation with many shareholders that offers its shares, which are traded on the stock market, to the general public

stock market
a market where shares are publicly traded

numbered company
a company that uses as its name the number assigned to it at the time of incorporation

incorporator
the person who signs and files the articles of incorporation

---

4 *Law Society Act*, RSO 1990, c. L.8, s. 61.0.7(1).

quickly and cannot wait to go through the process of incorporation. Numbered companies that are set up for this purpose are known as **shelf corporations**, or **shelf companies**. The company does not carry on any business—it is created for the sole purpose of being ready for someone who needs to start a company quickly.

If someone wants to give his or her corporation a name rather than a number, he or she must conduct a NUANS search to ensure that the name he or she wishes to use—or a similar name—is not already a registered name being used by another business. The NUANS search may reveal, for example, that the same name or a similar one is already being used by either a sole proprietor or a corporation. A NUANS search report must be submitted, together with an application for incorporation.

The name of a corporation must comply with the requirements, prohibitions, and restrictions that are set out in the *Business Names Act*, and in the regulation respecting names made under that Act. These are the same limitations and prescriptions governing the naming of sole proprietorships and partnerships that we discussed in Chapter 1.

Additional requirements for a corporation's name are the following:

- It cannot conflict with an existing corporate name.
- It cannot be a name that will deceive or confuse the public.
- It cannot include a name that is similar to another corporation or similar to a person not connected with the corporation.
- It cannot include an obscenity.

If a corporation incorporates as a numbered company, and later decides that it wants to be known to everyone and conduct business using an actual name, it can register the name as a **business style name**, or **trade name**. The corporation will be legally identified by its actual name, the numbered company name, but can otherwise run its business using the business style or trade name. For example, assume Bryce Aleem incorporated his business as 467262 Ontario Limited. If he decides that he now wants to be known to customers as "Bryce's Handyman Services," he can register this name under the *Business Names Act*, after conducting a NUANS search to ensure that the name can be used. Bryce's company will now be known as 467262 Ontario Limited "carrying on business" (or "cob") or "operating as" (or "o/a") Bryce's Handyman Services. Although Bryce can create business cards and advertise using the name "Bryce's Handyman Services," he must use the numbered company name (467262 Ontario Limited) for contracts and other legal matters.

Also, even if a corporation has an actual name, it can still register a business style name or trade name if it wants to operate its business using a different name. For example, if Eric incorporated a ski business called Eric's Best Skis Inc., and wants to open a separate location where he will also offer skiing lessons, he can register "Eric's Skiing Lessons" under the *Business Names Act* (assuming a NUANS search confirms that the name is available to use). He will then be known as Eric's Best Skis Inc., operating as (or carrying on business as) Eric's Skiing Lessons.

As mentioned above, the name of a corporation must end in "Limited," "Ltd.," "Corporation," "Corp.," "Incorporated," or "Inc." There is no legal distinction between any of these endings, and the incorporator is free to choose the one that he or she

shelf corporation/shelf company
a company that does not carry on any business and is created for the sole purpose of being available to someone who needs to start a company quickly

business style name/ trade name
the registered name—not the actual name of the corporation—that a company uses to conduct its business

prefers. It is mandatory to use one of them, so that anyone who deals with the business will know that it is incorporated and know, therefore, that the owners have limited liability. For example, assume a homeowner hires Bryce's Handyman Services Inc. to install hardwood floors and is dissatisfied with Bryce's work and wants to sue for damages. The company name, Bryce's Handyman Services Inc., makes it apparent that the proper party to sue is the company, and not Bryce personally. Even if Bryce was carrying on business using a trade name, he would be required to disclose his numbered company name when entering into contracts with his customers.

Articles of Incorporation

articles of incorporation
the legal document that sets out a corporation's purpose and that, when filed, creates the corporation

A corporation is created upon filing a legal document called the **articles of incorporation**. The individual who signs and files the articles of incorporation is known as the incorporator.

The articles of incorporation set out the purpose of a corporation and must include the following information:

- The name of the corporation. In the case of a numbered company, the name is listed as: _____ Ontario Limited. A number will be assigned when the incorporator files the articles of incorporation.
- The address of the registered office of the corporation.
- The name(s) of the director(s).
- The number of directors that the corporation is entitled to have. This can be expressed either as a fixed number or as a range of numbers, with a minimum number and a maximum number. A corporation may choose the latter option—a range of numbers—to allow for more flexibility.
- Any restrictions on the activities that the corporation may carry on.
- Any restrictions on the transfer of shares.
- The different classes of shares and, for each class, the authorized number of shares the corporation can issue.

The incorporator files the completed articles of incorporation (together with the filing fee) with the Companies and Personal Property Security Branch of the Ministry of Government Services.

Once filed, the articles of incorporation are assigned a corporation number and a date of incorporation. If the company is a numbered company, the number that is assigned—followed by the word "Ontario" and then by "Limited," "Incorporated," or "Corporation" or by their abbreviations ("Ltd.," "Inc.," or "Corp.")—will be the corporation's legal name.

In addition to filing the articles of incorporation, the incorporator must also file a form called a Form 1 Initial Return. This form provides the names and addresses of the directors and officers of the corporation and is required pursuant to the *Cor-*

Sample Articles of Incorporation

For Ministry Use Only
À l'usage exclusif du ministère

Ontario Corporation Number
Numéro de la société en Ontario

Articles of Incorporation
Statuts Constitutifs

Form 1
*Business
Corporations
Act*

Formule 1
*Loi sur les
sociétés par
actions*

1. The name of the corporation is: (Set out in BLOCK CAPITAL LETTERS)
   Dénomination sociale de la société : (Écrire en LETTRES MAJUSCULES SEULEMENT)

| B | R | Y | C | E | ' | S | | H | A | N | D | Y | M | A | N | | S | E | R | V | I | C | E | S | | I | N | C | . |

2. The address of the registered office is:
   Adresse du siège social :

   150 Seneca Road

   (Street & Number or R.R. Number & if Multi-Office Building give Room No.)
   (Rue et numéro ou numéro de la R.R. et, s'il s'agit d'un édifice à bureaux, numéro du bureau)

   Toronto   **ONTARIO** | M | 5 | M | 1 | N | 3 |

   (Name of Municipality or Post Office)   (Postal Code)
   (Nom de la municipalité ou du bureau de poste) (Code postal)

3. Number of directors is/are: Fixed number [   ]   **OR** minimum and maximum | 1 | 4 |
   Nombre d'administrateurs :   Nombre fixe   **OU** minimum et maximum

4. The first director(s) is/are:
   Premier(s) administrateur(s) :

First name, middle names and surname / Prénom, autres Prénoms et nom de famille	Address for service, giving Street & No. or R.R. No., Municipality, Province, Country and Postal Code / Domicile élu, y compris la rue et le numéro, le numéro de la R.R. ou le nom de la municipalité, la province, le pays et le code postal	Resident Canadian? Yes or No / Résident canadien? Oui/Non
Bryce Aleem	1954 Clumbed Avenue Toronto, ON M2N 1X5	Yes

5. Restrictions, if any, on business the corporation may carry on or on powers the corporation may exercise.
    Limites, s'il y a lieu, imposées aux activités commerciales ou aux pouvoirs de la société.

There are no restrictions.

6. The classes and any maximum number of shares that the corporation is authorized to issue:
    Catégories et nombre maximal, s'il y a lieu, d'actions que la société est autorisée à émettre :

An unlimited number of common shares.

7. Rights, privileges, restrictions and conditions (if any) attaching to each class of shares and directors authority with respect
    to any class of shares which may be issued in series:

    Droits, privilèges, restrictions et conditions, s'il y a lieu, rattachés à chaque catégorie d'actions et pouvoirs des
    administrateurs relatifs à chaque catégorie d'actions qui peut être émise en série :

    None.

8. The issue, transfer or ownership of shares is/is not restricted and the restrictions (if any) are as follows:
    L'émission, le transfert ou la propriété d'actions est/n'est pas restreint. Les restrictions, s'il y a lieu, sont les suivantes :

Shares issued by the Corporation shall not be transferred without the consent of either (i) the directors evidenced by a resolution passed or signed by them and recorded in the books of the Corporation or (ii) the holders of a majority in number of the outstanding voting shares of the Corporation.

9. Other provisions if any:
   Autres dispositions, s'il y a lieu :

(a) The number of shareholders of the Corporation, exclusive of persons who are in the employment of the Corporation or former shareholders of the Corporation who become shareholders during their employment with the Corporation, is limited to fifty (50), two or more persons holding one or more shares jointly being counted as one shareholder; and

(b) Any invitation to the public to subscribe for any securities of the Corporation is prohibited.

07116 (2008/06)

10. The names and addresses of the incorporators are:
   Noms et adresses des fondateurs :

First name, middle names and surname or corporate name Prénom, autres prénoms et nom de famille ou dénomination sociale	Full address for service or if a corporation, the address of the registered or head office giving street & No. or R.R. No., municipality, province, country and postal code Domicile élu au complet ou, dans le cas d'une société, adresse du siège social ou adresse de l'établissement principal, y compris la rue et le numéro ou le numéro de la R.R., la municipalité, la province, le pays et le code postal
Bryce Aleem	1954 Clumbed Avenue Toronto, ON M2N 1X5

These articles are signed in duplicate.
Les présents statuts sont signés en double exemplaire.

Full name(s) and signature(s) of incorporator(s). In the case of a corporation set out the name of the corporation and the name and office of the person signing on behalf of the corporation

Nom(s) au complet et signature(s) du ou des fondateurs. Si le fondateur est une société, indiquer la dénomination sociale et le nom et le titre de la personne signant au nom de la société

Bryce Aleem

_____
Signature / signature

Name of incorporator (or corporation name & signatories name and office)
Nom du fondateur (ou dénomination sociale et nom et titre du signataire)

_____
Signature / signature

Name of incorporator (or corporation name & signatories name and office)
Nom du fondateur (ou dénomination sociale et nom et titre du signataire)

_____
Signature / signature

Name of incorporator (or corporation name & signatories name and office)
Nom du fondateur (ou dénomination sociale et nom et titre du signataire)

_____
Signature / signature

Name of incorporator (or corporation name & signatories name and office)
Nom du fondateur (ou dénomination sociale et nom et titre du signataire)

porations Information Act.[5] If the information contained in the Form 1 changes, a new form with updated information must be filed.

Once the business is incorporated, the incorporator appoints someone to be the **first director** of the corporation. If it is decided, at the first shareholders' meeting, to keep the first director as a director, then he or she will be re-elected as a member of the **board of directors**. If, on the other hand, the decision is not to have the first director sit on the board of directors, the first director will not be re-elected.

When representing a client who wants to incorporate a business, a lawyer will often act as the incorporator and appoint him- or herself as the first director of the corporation. Proceeding in this way eliminates the need for the client to sign the articles of incorporation and therefore expedites the incorporation process. In this situation, the lawyer would not be re-elected as a director at the first shareholders' meeting. Lawyers use this method when creating a shelf corporation.

Organization: The Minute Book

After the articles of incorporation have been filed, it is time to get organized. This involves creating a **minute book**, which is used to store all of the corporation's important documents. A minute book should be kept in a safe location, such as the corporation's **registered head office** or the company's lawyer's office. A minute book will contain all the legal documents, including the following:

1. The articles of incorporation.
2. The rules or **bylaws** of the corporation, which describe how the company will be managed. Bylaws deal with matters affecting the day-to-day operation of the corporation and are easy to amend as required. There are typically two bylaws; the first one deals with the general conduct of the business, and the second one deals with borrowing money.

   Because bylaws are far easier and less expensive to amend than the articles of incorporation, the bylaws will typically contain much more detailed information about the operation of the corporation than the articles of incorporation do. In order to amend the articles of incorporation, the company has to register articles of amendment and pay a registration fee.
3. The **minutes** of the shareholders' meetings.
4. Shareholders' **resolutions**.
5. The minutes of the directors' meetings.
6. Directors' resolutions.
7. The shareholders' register, listing the names of the shareholders and their issued shares.
8. The directors' register, which lists (a) the name(s) of the directors, (b) the dates of their election, (c) the dates of their retirement, and (d) whether, as is sometimes the case, the directors have positions as **officers** in the com-

first director
the individual(s) appointed by the incorporator to act as a director until the first shareholders' meeting

board of directors
all of the directors of a corporation

minute book
the book containing all of the documents of the corporation

registered head office
the address of the corporation

bylaws
rules that govern the operation of a corporation

minutes
the written record of a shareholders' or directors' meeting

resolution
a decision made by a corporation's directors or shareholders

officer
an individual who manages the day-to-day functioning of a corporation

---

5 RSO 1990, c. C.39.

pany. If Bryce Aleem is both a director and the president of Helping Hands Inc., for example, this information will be on the directors' register.

corporate seal
a device, used to emboss paper, that confirms the authority of an individual to sign on behalf of the corporation

In the process of organizing itself, the corporation may also purchase a **corporate seal**, which is a device used to emboss a document. Embossing a document with a corporate seal proves that the person signing the document has the authority to sign on behalf of the corporation. Without such a seal, a person can prove authority to sign on behalf of the corporation by writing the following statement below his or her signature: "I have the authority to bind the corporation."

Parties to a Corporation

Every corporation must have at least one shareholder, one director, and one officer. (The roles and responsibilities of each position are discussed below.) Although these are all different positions, they may be filled by the same person if the corporation comprises only one person. For example, if Bryce Aleem incorporates a business on his own, he will be the only shareholder, the only director, and the only officer. If, on the other hand, Bryce incorporates together with Roger and Alonzo, the positions can be divided or shared among them. For example, they can all be directors and/or officers. Roger might be the president, Bryce the vice-president, and Alonzo the secretary treasurer. We discuss the different officer positions later in this chapter. If the three men each put money into the business, they will be shareholders as well. As you can see, someone can be a director, as well as an officer and/or a shareholder. A corporation can also hire employees. Employees are not directors, officers, or shareholders—they are simply employed by the corporation.

Shareholders

The shareholders are the actual owners of a corporation. A person (individual or corporation) becomes a shareholder when it/he/she purchases shares from the corporation or from an existing shareholder. Each **share** represents a unit of ownership, and a shareholder's percentage of ownership is determined by the number of shares it/he/she owns. The incorporator determines how many shares to issue, often after consulting with a financial adviser.

share
a unit of ownership in a corporation

For example, assume Bryce Aleem is the sole shareholder of 467262 Ontario Limited. He therefore owns 100 percent of the company. If the company issues only one share, then Bryce owns the one single share. If the company issues 100 shares, then Bryce would own all 100 shares. As this example illustrates, owning 100 percent of the company can mean having one share or 100 shares, depending on the number of shares the company issued. When determining a shareholder's interest in a company, the number of shares is not as relevant as the actual percentage of the issued shares.

share certificate
a written document that states the number of shares owned by a shareholder

Each shareholder receives a **share certificate** indicating the number of shares it/he/she owns. Shareholders are usually not involved in running the corporation. Instead, they have the right to vote at meetings, which are called shareholders' meetings. In this way, shareholders can have some control or influence over the day-to-day operation of the corporation. For example, it is the voting shareholders who elect the directors of the corporation.

Each shareholder is entitled to one vote for each share owned. Thus if Bryce Aleem owns one share, he is entitled to one vote; if Bryce Aleem owns 100 shares, he is entitled to 100 votes. The law requires the calling of "an annual meeting of shareholders not later than eighteen months after the corporation comes into existence and subsequently not later than fifteen months after holding the last preceding annual meeting."[6] At the annual meeting of shareholders, the shareholders will elect directors, appoint an auditor (or waive the appointment of an auditor), review the company's financial statements, and deal with any other business, as necessary.

Unless the bylaws provide otherwise, a shareholders' meeting is not valid without a **quorum**. This means that the majority of the shareholders who are entitled to vote (at least 51 percent) must be present at the meeting, either in person or by **proxy**. For example, if there are three voting shareholders, each of whom owns one share, two of the shareholders will constitute a quorum, because together they have two-thirds of the total shares, which is more than 51 percent. A shareholder who cannot attend a meeting can vote by mail or, alternatively, can appoint someone else to attend the meeting and vote on the shareholder's behalf. This is known as voting by proxy.

At a shareholders' meeting, decisions are made by passing resolutions. There are three types of resolutions—ordinary, special, and unanimous. **Ordinary resolutions** require a majority (51 percent) of all shareholder votes. Most decisions are made by ordinary resolutions. For example, electing a director and appointing an accountant are decisions that are made by an ordinary resolution of shareholders. **Special resolutions** require the approval of two-thirds of all shareholder votes. A special resolution is required for **fundamental changes** to the corporation.

Examples of fundamental changes include the following:

- amending the articles of incorporation,
- amending the bylaws,
- amalgamating the corporation with another corporation, and
- ending the corporation.

Unanimous resolutions require 100 percent of all shareholder votes. A decision not to appoint an **auditor**, for example, must be made by a unanimous resolution. Without it, a corporation must have an auditor.

A corporation can involve different types of shares. For example, many corporations have **common shares** and **preferred shares**. Common shares entitle their owners to voting rights, whereas preferred shares usually do not. The advantage of preferred shares, however, is that, in the event the corporation is dissolved, preferred shareholders are given priority over common shareholders and paid out first. There can also be different classes of shares, such as class A common shares and class B common shares, each class giving the various shareholders different rights within the corporation. For example, class A shares may give their owners the right to vote at shareholders' meetings, whereas class B shares do not involve this right.

quorum
the minimum number of people required to make a decision

proxy
the document that permits a shareholder to vote by mail or to appoint someone else to attend the meeting and vote on the shareholder's behalf

ordinary resolution
a decision made by a majority (at least 51 percent) of all shareholder votes

special resolution
a decision made by two-thirds of all shareholder votes

fundamental change
a change that will affect the corporation and that requires two-thirds of all shareholder votes

unanimous resolution
a decision about the corporation that requires 100 percent of all shareholder votes

auditor
a person appointed by a corporation to oversee its financial matters

common shares
a class of shares that typically include the right to vote

preferred shares
a class of shares that typically give their owners the right to be paid out before the owners of common shares are paid out

---

6 *Business Corporations Act*, s. 94(1)(a).

Even if a corporation has only one shareholder, it may still create different classes of shares. This is to ensure that any new shareholders don't have the same rights as the initial shareholder.

To illustrate, let's say that when Bryce Aleem incorporated his business on his own, he set up two classes of common shares, class A and class B, and issued himself one class A common share. If, in the future, Bryce brings in another shareholder, he can make sure the new shareholder doesn't have the same rights as he does by issuing the new shareholder the class B common shares.

If the corporation is a public company, shares are traded freely on the open market and there is no restriction on a shareholder's right to sell its/his/her shares. If the corporation is a private company, then ownership is private and shares are issued only to the owners. Because a private company does not issue shares to the public, there will likely be restrictions in the articles of incorporation on a shareholder's right to sell shares. The incorporator of a private company will restrict the issuance and the transfer of shares in the articles of incorporation, to ensure that strangers do not end up becoming a shareholder of the incorporator's private business. For example, let's say that when Bryce Aleem incorporates as the sole owner and shareholder of 467262 Ontario Limited, he wants to ensure that, if he ever decides to have other owners or shareholders in his business, he will have the right to choose who they will be. In the event that he later issues a share to his brother-in-law Joe, for example, the restriction on the transfer of shares will prevent Joe from selling his share to a stranger.

There is no limit on the number of shareholders a public company may have. A private company, on the other hand, can have no more than 50 shareholders. As mentioned above, shareholders receive payment in the form of a dividend for their investment in a corporation. A dividend represents a share of the corporation's profits, and the amount of the dividend is proportionate to the shareholder's interest in the corporation. For example, if Bryce Aleem owns 100 percent of the shares of 467262 Ontario Limited, his dividend will represent 100 percent of the total dividend payment.

Directors

The directors of a corporation are the individuals who manage, or supervise the management of, the corporation. Every private corporation must have at least one director. The articles of incorporation will set out who the initial or first directors are, but the shareholders will then formally elect the directors at their first annual meeting, which must occur within 18 months of incorporation. If the intention is to elect directors who are not the individuals named in the articles of incorporation— as in the case of a shelf corporation, for example—the first meeting will take place much sooner. The maximum term of a director is three years, which can be renewed. The legal requirements regarding directors are that a director

- must be an individual,
- must be at least 18 years old,

- must not be bankrupt, and
- must not be of unsound mind.

Another legal requirement for Canadian corporations is that at least 25 percent of the directors must be Canadian residents.

The directors as a group (even if there is only one director) form the board of directors, who are responsible for managing the corporation in accordance with the provisions in the articles of incorporation. The directors must approve the **financial statements** of the corporation to ensure that the business is being run in a financially responsible manner. Directors are not required also to be shareholders of the corporation.

As mentioned above, private companies must have at least one director, and often they have only one. Public companies must have at least three directors. The articles of incorporation or the bylaws of the corporation may provide how and when meetings of directors will take place. If there is only one director, a meeting can be as simple as the sole director signing a **written resolution**. If there is more than one director, there will likely be a formal meeting. Unlike shareholders, a director cannot give his or her proxy to a third party. In other words, a director must attend a directors' meeting; he or she cannot authorize someone else to attend on his or her behalf. There must be a quorum before decisions can be made at a directors' meeting. The articles of incorporation or the bylaws may state the number of directors that will constitute a quorum at a directors' meeting. However, if the corporation has fewer than three directors, then all directors must be present at a directors' meeting in order to make a quorum possible.

A director has a duty of trust to the corporation and to its shareholders, known as a **fiduciary duty**. This means that a director has a duty to act honestly, in good faith, and in the best interests of the corporation, and must put the corporation's interests ahead of his or her own interests. Their fiduciary duty requires directors to avoid a **conflict of interest**. For example, assume that the director of a corporation hires Eric, the owner of Eric's Renovation Services, to renovate the corporation's head office, and Eric happens to be the director's boyfriend. Many might consider this to be a conflict of interest and think that the director chose Eric not because he is a skilled and talented renovator, but because he is the director's boyfriend.

Another example of a conflict of interest might be a case where the corporation is looking to buy land, and the director recommends a piece of land that he or she happens to own. Although that particular land may be a desirable purchase for the corporation, the purchase might be perceived as a conflict of interest because of the personal benefit it would bring to the director. **Insider trading** is an example of a conflict of interest that can happen in a public corporation. It occurs when a director has access to non-public material information about an investment and uses this inside information to his or her advantage by, for example, selling his or her shares in an investment that is expected to decline in value. The conflict of interest consists in the fact that the director has this information only because of his or her position in the company.

financial statement
a written report, usually prepared by an accountant, that provides details about the financial aspects of the corporation

written resolutions
decisions that the corporation's directors or shareholders make in writing instead of at a formal meeting

fiduciary duty
the duty to act honestly, in good faith, and in the best interests of someone or something (such as a corporation)

conflict of interest
occurs when a person in a position of trust has a conflict between his/her personal interests and his/her professional interests

insider trading
when the director of a corporation has access to non-public material information about an investment and uses this inside information to his or her advantage

In addition to their fiduciary duty, directors also have a duty of care, which is the duty to act with the care, diligence, and skill that a reasonably prudent person would exercise in directing the company.

Officers

The officers of a corporation are appointed by the director(s). Officers are responsible for running the day-to-day business of the corporation. The most common types of appointed officers in a corporation are the following:

- president,
- vice-president (a corporation may have more than one of these—for example, there may be a vice-president of operations as well as a vice-president of sales),
- secretary, and
- treasurer (a position often combined with that of the secretary and called the secretary-treasurer).

It is very common, especially in small corporations, to have one person acting as both the director and the officer. It is also common to have one person holding several officer positions. Officers are not required to be shareholders of the corporation.

Figure 3.1   Parties to a Corporation

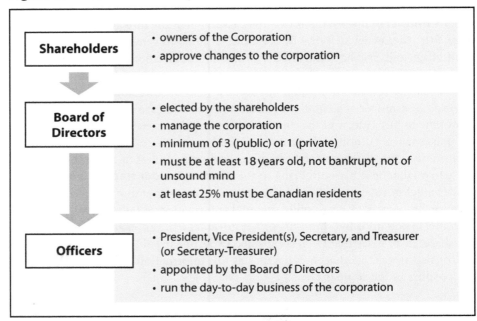

Figure 3.2 Checklist: Things to Consider Before Incorporating

Things to Consider	Options
Name of corporation	Conduct a NUANS search if not using a numbered company.
Trade name or business style name	Is a trade name (or business style name) desired for a numbered company or as an alternate name for a named company?
Who will incorporate?	Will a lawyer or a first director incorporate?
Who will be the director(s)?	Will it be one director or multiple directors? The number can be fixed, or a range of numbers can be established to allow for future changes.
Restrictions on activities	Will the corporation's range of activities be limited?
Classes of shares	Will there be one class of share or multiple classes (with each class conferring different rights on the shareholders)?
Restrictions on transfer of shares	Will there be restrictions on the transfer of shares, to prevent strangers from becoming shareholders?
Who will be the officer(s)?	What are the names and positions of the officers?

Amalgamation

Amalgamation occurs when two or more corporations combine to form one corporation. All the assets and liabilities of the corporations that are amalgamating in this way will become the assets and liabilities of the new amalgamated corporation. In order for corporations to amalgamate, they must all be governed by the same legislation. In other words, a provincially incorporated company cannot amalgamate with a federally incorporated company, unless further steps are taken to bring the two companies under the same jurisdiction.

When corporations amalgamate, the new corporation thus created can use the name of any of the corporations involved in the amalgamation. If the new amalgamated corporation wants to use a different name, however, a NUANS search must be conducted to determine whether or not that name is already being used. For example, if Buddy's Boots Inc. and Ash's Shoes Corp. decide to amalgamate, they can call their new amalgamated corporation either Buddy's Boots Inc. or Ash's Shoes Corp. However, if they want to use the name Buddy and Ash Footwear Limited, they will need to conduct a NUANS search to make sure the name is available and permitted. Corporations amalgamate by filing **articles of amalgamation** with the Ministry of Government Services.

articles of amalgamation
the document that must be registered when two corporations amalgamate (join)

Once the articles of amalgamation are registered, they are deemed to be the articles of incorporation of the newly amalgamated company.

The amalgamating corporations must enter into a written amalgamation agreement, which the shareholders of each corporation must approve by a special resolution.

Dissolving a Corporation

Unlike a natural person, a corporation never dies. A corporation can therefore exist indefinitely, unless it is dissolved. The four ways to dissolve a corporation are as follows:

1. *Voluntary dissolution.* A decision to voluntarily dissolve a corporation requires a vote of the shareholders by special resolution after they have received notice of the corporation's intent to dissolve. The corporation must pay all debts, liabilities, and taxes before distributing the corporate assets to the shareholders. Finally, the corporation must file **articles of dissolution**.

2. *Dissolution for non-compliance.* A certificate of incorporation may be cancelled if the corporation has committed certain acts, including the following:

   - failing to have the required number of directors,
   - failing to meet the residency requirements for directors,
   - being convicted of a criminal offence, or
   - the corporation has acted or may act in a way that is oppressive or unfairly prejudicial to a security holder, creditor, director, or officer.[7]

3. *Voluntary winding up.* If the corporation becomes bankrupt or insolvent, the shareholders can decide, by special resolution, to terminate the corporation and have an outside liquidator or trustee wind up the corporation. The trustee will be responsible for providing a full accounting to the shareholders. This process is governed by the *Bankruptcy and Insolvency Act*.[8]

4. *Court-ordered winding up.* Upon an application made by the corporation or by one of its shareholders, the court may order an outsider (someone who is not a party to the corporation) to wind up the corporation under **judicial** supervision. This is similar to a voluntary winding up except that, in the case of a court-ordered winding up, the court monitors the entire process.

Shareholder Remedies

Shareholders who are unhappy with the corporation's management, or who feel they are being mistreated by the corporation, have several remedies available to them under both the provincial and federal legislation that governs corporations. The most common remedy is the **oppression remedy**. This remedy permits a shareholder to apply to the court for relief if the shareholder feels that the corporation's

articles of dissolution
the document that must be registered when a corporation voluntarily dissolves (closes down)

judicial
the authority of a court

oppression remedy
a remedy, available to shareholders, that permits a shareholder to apply to the court for relief if the shareholder feels that the actions of the corporation—or any use of the directors' powers—have been oppressive or unfairly prejudicial

---

7 *Business Corporations Act*, s. 240.

8 RSC 1985, c. B-3.

actions or any use of the directors' powers has been oppressive or unfairly prejudicial. The court may make any order it deems appropriate, including an order dissolving the corporation. This remedy is also available to directors, creditors, and officers of the corporation.

A second remedy available to shareholders is the **derivative action**. This is a statutory remedy that permits a shareholder to seek **leave** to bring an action, in the name of the corporation, against a director (or directors) whose actions are a concern to the shareholder. What is the rationale for this remedy? If the directors are breaching their fiduciary duty to the corporation, they are not likely to bring an action against themselves for breach of their own duty. This remedy permits a shareholder to enforce the directors' fiduciary duty to the corporation when the directors themselves are not willing to do so.

A third remedy available to shareholders is to obtain a court order directing an investigation into the activities of the corporation.

derivative action
a remedy, available to shareholders, that permits a shareholder to bring an action in the name of the corporation

leave
permission of the court

Unanimous Shareholder Agreement

A unanimous shareholder agreement is an agreement among *all* shareholders of the corporation that restricts the directors' powers with respect to the management of the corporation. The purpose of this type of agreement is to give shareholders control over the matters dealt with in the agreement. By taking power away from the directors, the shareholders are, in essence, acting as directors. As such, they will have the same liability as directors and can be sued if, for example, they breach their fiduciary duty to the corporation.

If there is a unanimous shareholder agreement, it will be binding on any new shareholder who invests in the company. This ensures that unanimity is preserved, which is a key feature of this type of shareholder agreement.

Liability of a Corporation

As already mentioned, a corporation is a legal entity in and of itself, separate from its shareholders, directors, and officers. In other words, the law regards the corporation as a legal person. This means that a corporation is responsible for its own actions and will have liability in tort, criminal, and contract law. Even though the corporation itself cannot think and behave like a human person, the courts use the **identification theory of corporate liability** to impose liability on the corporation. According to this theory, a corporation is liable when the person who commits a tort or crime is the "directing mind" of the corporation. For example, a corporation will be liable for its directors' actions.

A corporation will also be liable for breach of any contracts that were entered into by an agent of the corporation, as long as the agent was acting with proper authority on behalf of the corporation.

identification theory of corporate liability
the theory used to describe the liability of a corporation when the person who commits a tort or crime is the "directing mind" of the corporation

Advantages of Incorporating

The main advantage of incorporating is that it limits liability. Because a corporation is regarded as a separate person in the eyes of the law, the shareholders cannot lose more than their initial investment, and the shareholders, directors, and officers will not be personally liable for the actions of the corporation. The other advantages of incorporating include the following:

- Flexibility—can offer different degrees of ownership and profit sharing;
- Availability of capital—enables the business to raise capital more easily from creditors, which may be more comfortable lending to a corporation than to an individual;
- Continuous existence—unlike humans, corporations don't die;
- Tax advantages—corporations are taxed more favourably than individuals;
- Easy transferral of ownership—can be transferred simply by selling shares, if permitted by the articles of incorporation.

Disadvantages of Incorporating

Disadvantages of incorporating include the following:

- More expensive and complicated to incorporate a business than to establish a sole proprietorship or partnership;
- Relatively extensive regulation and record-keeping involved;
- Potential for losing control of the business depending on the number of shares issued;
- Tax reporting is more complicated—the corporation must file a separate tax return;
- Potential for conflict between directors and shareholders.

Provincial Corporations and Federal Corporations

A corporation can be provincial or federal depending on how it was created. A provincial corporation is created by provincial legislation. In Ontario, this is the *Business Corporations Act*. A federal corporation is created by the *Canada Business Corporations Act*. The decision whether to incorporate provincially or federally depends on the corporation's main objectives and the nature of its business.

Most small companies that carry on business in Ontario will incorporate provincially. An Ontario corporation can even operate in another province by obtaining an **extra-provincial licence**.

extra-provincial licence
a licence that authorizes a corporation to conduct its business in another province

The only reason a corporation needs to incorporate federally is if it wants to operate throughout Canada or to conduct business outside of Canada. Many countries will deal with a Canadian business only if it is a federal corporation. The name of a federally incorporated company will be recognized everywhere in Canada except Quebec, where the French version of the name must be registered.

The process of incorporating provincially is much simpler and, overall, less expensive than incorporating federally. There are additional filing requirements for federal corporations, and a name is more difficult to obtain because the database is not provincial but Canada-wide.

KEY TERMS

articles of amalgamation, 39
articles of dissolution, 40
articles of incorporation, 26
auditor, 35
board of directors, 33
business style name/trade name, 25
bylaws, 33
common shares, 35
conflict of interest, 37
corporate seal, 34
derivative action, 41
dividend, 22
extra-provincial licence, 42
fiduciary duty, 37
financial statement, 37
first director, 33
fundamental change, 35

identification theory of
  corporate liability, 41
incorporate, 22
incorporator, 24
insider trading, 37
judicial, 40
leave, 41
limited liability, 22
minute book, 33
minutes, 33
not-for-profit corporation, 23
numbered company, 24
officer, 33
oppression remedy, 40
ordinary resolution, 35
piercing the corporate veil
  (or lifting the corporate veil), 23

plaintiff, 22
preferred shares, 35
private corporation, 24
proxy, 35
public corporation, 24
quorum, 35
registered head office, 33
resolution, 33
sham, 23
share, 34
share certificate, 34
shareholder, 22
shelf corporation/shelf company, 25
special resolution, 35
stock market, 24
unanimous resolution, 35
written resolutions, 37

REVIEW QUESTIONS

1. Who owns a corporation? *shareholders*

2. What is the most significant difference between a corporation and any other type of business organization? *the law treat one business as 1 etti and the*

3. What does "piercing the corporate veil" mean? Provide an example of when piercing the corporate veil would occur. *Court will exposed responable the shareholders so they will be res*

4. What are the three main types of corporations? *Business non prov, professio*

5. Is "123456 Ontario" a valid name for a corporation? Explain your answer. *NO its missing the Inc.*

6. Can a corporation ever use a name that is not its registered name? Explain your answer. *yes all the legal doc will have to make it clear*

7. List three items that are included in the articles of incorporation. *name, address, any ristrictants*

8. What is a corporate seal? Is it mandatory for a corporation to use one?
no its not mandatory, to Use one Comporate seal is a seal with the Corporation logo.

9. What is a share certificate? *shareholder*

10. ABC Company has 20 voting shareholders, and each shareholder owns one common share. At a shareholders' meeting, how many shareholders constitutes a quorum? *51% 11%*

11. Do shareholders have to attend a meeting in person in order to vote? Explain your answer. *No you can vote by proxy*

12. Ari Michaels is the director of DEF Limited. DEF Limited wants to purchase land to expand its manufacturing plant. Ari, together with his brother Elliott, owns property that is suitable for this purpose. Is there any reason that Ari, as a director of DEF, should not purchase this property for the corporation?

13. If Ari, the sole director of DEF Limited, dies, what happens to the corporation? *it will dissolve or was a written aareemer that say otherwise.*

PART II

Property Law

Chapters 4, 5, and 6 of this text deal with various types of property law: personal property, real property, and intellectual property. In Chapter 4, we discuss real property—in other words, land and everything permanently attached to land, such as a house. We explain how real property rights arise, and we describe the legal implications of owning this type of property. We also explain how ownership of real property differs from ownership of any other type of property. Chapter 5 deals with mortgages, which involve borrowing money and using real property as security for the loan. Chapter 6 deals with intellectual property, which is an intangible property right that protects creations of the mind. We explain the different types of intellectual property and discuss the rights associated with this form of property.

Real Property Law

4

LEARNING OUTCOMES

After reading this chapter, you should be able to:

- Understand the meaning of real property and the principles of land ownership

- Understand the different estates and interests in land

- Describe how interests in land are created

- Understand the concept of adverse possession and of interests created by prescription

- Explain how co-owners of a property hold title to land

- Understand the different land registration systems in Ontario

- Describe what a title search involves

- Explain the advantages of title insurance

Introduction

Real property is the legal term used to describe land and everything that is attached to land, including

real property
land, including everything
that is attached to it

- minerals below the surface of the land,
- airspace above the land,
- buildings on the land, and
- **fixtures** on the land (or within any buildings situated on the land).

fixtures
chattels that have become
attached or affixed to
real property; immovable
possessions attached
to real property

As this list suggests, real property does not include any unattached movable items of property, such as a desk, a lawn chair, or a computer. These items are called **personal property**, or **chattels**. Once a chattel is permanently attached to real property, however, it becomes a fixture. For example, a storage shed that sits on top of the land is a chattel; it can easily be moved. However, if the storage shed is installed in the ground using concrete, it becomes a fixture.

personal property
chattels; property that
is not real property

The degree to which personal property is attached to the land will determine whether or not it is a chattel or a fixture. The distinction is important because the law treats chattels and fixtures differently. For example, when someone purchases real property, fixtures are deemed to be included in the purchase, and chattels are deemed not to be included. In a home purchase, for example, the kitchen cabinets and counters, doors, railings, and any other fixtures will all be included in the purchase price. The kitchen table and chairs will not be included, however, because they are chattels.

chattels
movable possessions not
attached to real property

The contract between a buyer and a seller of real property is called the **agreement of purchase and sale**. The "buyer" is sometimes known as the "purchaser," and the "seller" as the "vendor." In this text, we use these terms interchangeably.

The agreement of purchase and sale is used in purchases of any type of real property, such as

agreement of
purchase and sale
a contract between
a buyer (purchaser)
and seller (vendor)
of real property

- a house,
- a vacant piece of land, or
- a condominium unit.

The buyer and seller will negotiate in the agreement what fixtures and chattels to include in the purchase. The general rule is that fixtures are included unless the agreement specifically excludes them, and chattels are excluded unless the agreement specifically includes them. For example, if the buyer wants certain chattels included in the agreement, such as the kitchen table and chairs, or an area rug, the buyer can ask the seller to include them. Similarly, if the seller wants to remove certain fixtures, such as the dining-room chandelier or antique doorknobs, he or she can exclude them in the agreement.

estate
an interest in land that
provides the right to
exclusive possession

Real property law dates back to feudal times in England. Much of the terminology in use today dates back to that time. In feudal times, the King of England owned all land, and granted some of his subjects **estates** in land, or the right to use the land, in return for their service and allegiance. The King had the right to **forfeit**

forfeit
lose the right

(take back) the land if, for example, the subject committed treason or some other wrongful act. This was known as the feudal system.

The English law of real property came to Ontario with the English colonists. Today, the Crown is still the ultimate owner of all Ontario land. This means that the government controls the use, disposition, and development of all land in Ontario. For example, municipal governments regularly pass **bylaws** restricting the use to which land and buildings can be put, and regulating the size, shape, and location of all buildings and structures that are situated on the land. The government also has the right to **expropriate** (take ownership of) land if it is required for the public good. For example, the government might need someone's land in order to widen an existing road or to build a new one. The government will compensate a landowner whose land it has expropriated by paying the landowner the **fair market value** of the property. The Crown will thereby reacquire ownership of the expropriated land.

Another example of the Crown's ultimate ownership rights to all land is the **doctrine of escheat**. This doctrine provides that if a landowner dies without a will and without any heirs (anyone entitled to inherit the landowner's property), the land **escheats** (reverts back) to the Crown.

Because the Crown is the ultimate owner of all land, and because land is permanent and immovable, owning land is different than owning other kinds of property. Land ownership is closer to "possession" of land than it is to absolute ownership; it involves rights and obligations that are recognized and enforced by law. Indeed, individuals don't own land; rather they own estates or **interests in land**. The rights that a person has with respect to his or her land will depend upon what estate or interest he or she has in the land.

Estates in Land

An estate in land represents the extent of a person's rights with respect to the land, and it includes the right to **exclusive possession** of the land. There are three types of estates in land:

1. the **fee simple estate**,
2. the **life estate**, and
3. the **leasehold estate**.

Fee Simple Estate

The fee simple estate is the form of ownership in land that is closest to absolute ownership. The Crown grants the fee simple estate to the first "owner" by way of Crown patent.

In theory, the fee simple estate extends physically upwards into the sky directly above the land and downwards, below the land, to the centre of the earth. In practice, there are limitations in both directions. Looking up, a landowner cannot sue airplanes flying overhead for trespass, although the owner could sue someone who begins to make permanent use of the owner's airspace by, for example, building a

bylaws (municipal)
laws that are passed by a municipality

expropriate
reacquire land while compensating the owners; something the Crown is entitled to do for public purposes

fair market value
the amount that property would sell for in the open market

doctrine of escheat
a common-law doctrine providing that if a landowner dies without a will and without heirs to inherit his or her land, the land will revert to the Crown

escheats
the reversion of property to the Crown

interests in land
rights to use someone else's land that are not estates and do not confer a right to exclusive possession of the land

exclusive possession
sole possession of the land; denial of possession to all others

fee simple estate
the right to exclusive possession and the right to dispose of the land for an indefinite period of time; most absolute form of ownership

life estate
a person's right to exclusive possession of the property for the length of his or her life

leasehold estate
the right to exclusive possession of the property for a specified period of time in return for the payment of rent

structure that overhangs the owner's property. The same applies to subterranean ownership; most Crown patents do not include oil and mineral rights. These are reserved for the Crown.

A person with a fee simple estate (this person is called "the owner in fee simple") has the right to exclusive possession of the land and the right to dispose of the land for an indefinite period of time. This person is considered to be the true owner of the land and has all the rights associated with land ownership. These rights include the right to

- grant the fee simple estate to someone else (by sale or gift),
- grant a life estate in the property (discussed below),
- grant a leasehold estate in the property (discussed below), or
- convey the property by inheritance (with or without a will).

These rights are subject to the Crown's ability to acquire land by way of expropriation, to the doctrine of escheat, and to the restrictions and limitations imposed by municipal bylaws.

Life Estate

A life estate gives its owner the right to exclusive possession of the property for the duration of his or her lifetime. When someone with a life estate dies, the life estate ends and the right to possession of the property reverts to the person who holds the estate in fee simple. For example, assume that Jose has a fee simple estate in real property, and he grants a life estate in that land to his mother, Francesca. During her lifetime, Francesca has the right to exclusive possession of the land. When she dies, however, the property will revert back to Jose, because he holds the estate in fee simple.

The owner in fee simple can convey a life estate to one person and the fee simple estate to another. For example, a man can transfer a life estate in his house to his mother, and the fee simple estate to his son. Although the son has been made the owner in fee simple, he will not have any right to possession of the house until his grandmother dies.

life tenant
the owner of a life estate

remainderman
the term used to refer to the owner in fee simple who must wait until a life estate ends before acquiring possession of a property

Once a life estate is created, both the owner of the life estate (also known as the **life tenant**) and the owner of the fee simple (also known as the **remainderman**) have legal rights to the same property. The life estate holder has the right to exclusive possession during his or her lifetime, while the fee simple holder has the right of ownership and the right to reacquire the right of possession to the property as soon as the life tenant dies. In other words, the fee simple holder is not entitled to possession of the property until the life tenant dies and the life estate ends. The fee simple holder can, however, sell or gift the property to someone else while the life tenant still has possession. In this situation, the new owner will hold the fee simple estate in the property but will not be entitled to possession of it until the life tenant dies.

commit waste
destroy, abuse, or make permanent undesirable changes to real property

A life tenant is responsible for maintaining the real property, which includes paying realty taxes, insuring the property, and paying the interest portion of mortgage payments. He or she must use the land in a reasonable manner, and must not **commit waste** on the land. For example, he or she must not tear down buildings or destroy trees. Basically, a life tenant has the right of possession during his or her lifetime only and must preserve the property for the owner in fee simple.

The person with the fee simple estate in land may grant successive life estates in that same parcel of land. For example, assume that David grants a life estate first to Bob, then to Chuck, and then to Don. When Bob dies, Chuck gets a life estate in the property. When Chuck dies, Don gets a life estate in the property. When Don dies, David will regain possession of the property (assuming that he is still alive).

The owner of a life estate in land may in turn grant the right to possession of the land to someone else, but that right to possession will end when the life tenant dies. For example, assume that David is the owner in fee simple of a property that has a townhouse. He grants Sam a life estate in the property. Sam in turn grants Alice the right to exclusive possession of the townhouse. As soon as Sam dies, the life estate ends, and the right to possession reverts to David. Life estates are rarely used anymore. The fee simple estate is by far the most common estate granted.

Leasehold Estate

A leasehold estate grants the right to exclusive possession of the property for a specified period of time, in return for the payment of rent. This estate creates a landlord–tenant relationship between the parties.

For example, assume that Elana has the fee simple estate in a townhouse property and grants a leasehold estate to Aaron. Both Elana and Aaron will have legal rights to the same property. Aaron, the tenant, is entitled to exclusive possession of the property during the term of the leasehold agreement and must pay rent to Elana, the landlord. Elana is entitled to regain possession of the property only when the tenancy is terminated.

Condominiums

Condominiums are not a separate estate in land but are included here because they are a type of fee simple ownership. The owner of a condominium unit owns the fee simple estate of that unit and, in addition, shares ownership of all the common areas of the building, such as the hallways, the lobby, the elevator, and the recreational facilities.

Figure 4.1   Estates in Land

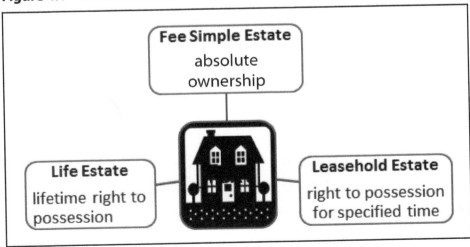

Interests in Land

Interests in land provide the right to *use* someone else's land, but not the right to exclusive possession of that land.

Easements

An **easement** gives a person the right to use a portion of someone else's land for a specific purpose. An easement is often referred to as a **right of way**.

> **easement**
> the right to use a portion of someone else's land for a specific purpose, without requiring the owner's permission each time the land is used

For example, assume that Keith and Adam are neighbours and share a single driveway that leads to a garage behind each of their homes. Each owns the part of the driveway that is situated on his own land. In addition, each has an easement interest over the other's land—that is, the right to use the other's part of the driveway in order to access his own garage. See Figure 4.2.

> **right of way**
> the right to use a portion of another's land for access purposes

The land that provides the easement is called the **servient tenement** and the land that benefits from the easement is called the **dominant tenement**. In Figure 4.2, assume that Adam owns property A, which includes easement #1, and Keith owns property B, which includes easement #2. For easement #1, property A is the servient tenement and property B is the dominant tenement. For easement #2, property B is the servient tenement and property A is the dominant tenement.

> **servient tenement**
> land over which an easement runs

> **dominant tenement**
> land that benefits from an easement

Figure 4.2   A Mutual Easement

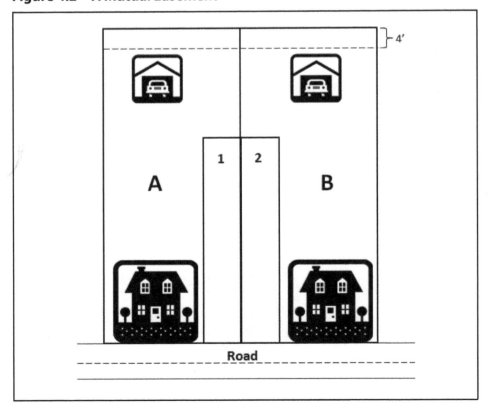

Easement interests attach to the land, not to the owner. In other words, if Keith sells his property (property B) to Mary, Mary has the right to use easement #1, and cannot prevent Adam from using easement #2. This type of easement is created by **express grant**—in other words, by agreement between the owner of the servient tenement and the owner of the dominant tenement.

The easement illustrated in Figure 4.2 is a mutual easement. In such a case, as you can see, each property is both a dominant tenement and a servient tenement.

Easements that are not mutual will have only one dominant tenement and one servient tenement. For example, an easement right in favour of Bell Canada or a utility company typically exists over the rear four feet of many properties in Ontario. This easement permits Bell Canada or the utility company to use someone's land in order to access wiring or utility poles, as necessary.

In Figure 4.2, assume that Bell Canada has an easement over the rear four feet of Adam's and Keith's property. Bell Canada can access that part of Adam's and Keith's property without their permission. Properties A and B are servient tenements and Bell Canada is a dominant tenement.

Easements can also be created by **prescription**. This means that the easement is created by the passage of time and not by express grant. Easements by prescription are discussed below, in the section on adverse interests in land.

The owner of a servient tenement cannot do anything to obstruct an easement. For example, Adam cannot park his car on the mutual driveway, and thereby prevent Keith from using the driveway to get to his garage. Also, Adam cannot build a permanent shed on the rear four feet of his property and thereby obstruct the utility easement.

Encroachments

An **encroachment** is any building or structure that intrudes upon someone else's property. A common example is an overhanging roof, or the eaves of a building that is situated too close to the property line. Another example of an encroachment is a shed or fence that ends up being partly or wholly built on the lands of a neighbour. In this situation, the neighbour can insist that the structure (or the part of it that is extending onto his property) be removed.

However, an owner of land who permits an encroachment to exist for 20 years may lose the right to object to the encroachment. (See the discussion of adverse interests in land, below.)

The owner of an encroaching structure can preserve his or her encroachment interest by entering into an **encroachment agreement** with the owner of the adjoining land (the land subject to the encroachment) upon registration of this agreement. The encroachment interest will then attach to the land, and the encroaching structure can remain, regardless of who owns the property. The agreement thus also clears up title on the property and avoids future problems regarding title.

express grant
creation of an easement by written document from the owner of the servient tenement to the owner of the dominant tenement

prescription
the means by which an interest is acquired in someone else's land after a period of open and uninterrupted use

encroachment
a building or structure intruding upon someone else's land

encroachment agreement
an agreement between neighbours that deals with an encroachment issue and clears up title

Restrictive Covenants

restrictive covenant
a promise by an owner of
land to refrain from doing
something on the property

A **restrictive covenant** imposes restrictions on the use of the property. It is a promise made by an owner to refrain from doing something on his or her property. The
restrictions are registered on title and are therefore binding on all subsequent owners.
An example of a restrictive covenant would be a restriction against parking a boat
on a driveway or against installing a giant satellite dish.

The restriction must be reasonable in nature and cannot be contrary to the public
interest in order to be enforceable. It must also be *negative in nature*, which means
that it is a promise *not* to do something, as opposed to a promise to do something.
For example, "all front doors must be painted red" is not a restrictive covenant, because it is stating what must be done, as opposed to what must not be done. "Front
doors must not be painted green," on the other hand, is a valid restrictive covenant.

Builders often use restrictive covenants in subdivision developments to maintain
control over the appearance of homes at the time that a subdivision is being created,
with the goal of creating an aesthetically desirable neighbourhood. These restrictive
covenants will bind the purchasers and all future owners.

Adverse Interests in Land

adverse interest in land
an interest in someone
else's land that is acquired
by using that person's land,
without permission, for a
certain period of time

An **adverse interest in land** is acquired by using another person's land, without
permission, for a certain period of time. The act of using another person's land adversely (that is, without invitation or permission) creates a permanent right to use
that land. The three types of adverse interests we discuss here are the following:

1. adverse possession,
2. an easement interest created by prescription, and
3. an encroachment interest created by prescription.

Registry System
a land registration system
in Ontario governed
by the *Registry Act*

Land Titles System
a land registration system
in Ontario governed
by the *Land Titles Act*

It is important to note that adverse interest claims exist only in the **Registry
System** and not in the **Land Titles System**. These two systems of land registration
are discussed later in this chapter.

Adverse Possession

adversely
without the owner's
permission

extinguished
brought to an end

adverse possession
valid title to land acquired
through open, visible, and
uninterrupted possession
of that property, without
the owner's permission, for
a period of at least 10 years

It is possible to acquire the right to the fee simple estate in someone else's land
simply by using the land as if it were your own, over a long period of time. If a person
exercises exclusive possession of another person's property **adversely** (without the
owner's permission), openly and continuously, the original owner's interest in that
portion of the land that was used will be **extinguished** after 10 years of uninterrupted use, and the person who has used the land will obtain the fee simple estate.
This is called **adverse possession**.

For example, assume that Allan maintains a vegetable garden on land that is
owned by Brian. Allan takes care of the garden for many years. Brian never tends to
the garden, and never uses the property. Although Brian knows about the garden on
his land, he neither consents to it nor does anything to stop it. After 10 years, Allan

will acquire a valid claim to that piece of land by adverse possession, and Brian will lose the right to regain possession of the land. The period of possession must be continuous and undisputed. If the true owner of the land regains possession at any time during the 10 years, the time period stops running. For example, Brian can stop the 10 years from running by simply using the property himself, even for a short period of time, or by telling Allan he can no longer use it.

Adverse possession claims attach to the land, not to the owner. For example, if Allan sells his property to Nancy after using the garden on Brian's land for six years, and Nancy continues to use the garden, uninterrupted, without consent and exclusively, for four more years, she will acquire the right to that piece of Brian's land.

Easement by Prescription

The second adverse interest is an **easement by prescription**. It is possible to acquire an easement interest by prescription if the following conditions are met:

- The easement has been used openly and continuously for at least 20 years (there can be different owners during this 20-year period).
- The owner of the servient tenement knows that the easement is being used.
- The owner of the servient tenement has not consented to the use of the easement.
- The owner of the servient tenement has not received any payment for the use of his/her land.

easement by prescription
an easement right to someone else's land that is acquired after a period of open and uninterrupted use

In the case of an easement by prescription, the easement is imposed by law on the owner of the servient tenement. The owner of the servient tenement is entitled to prevent the use of his or her property at any time during the 20-year period, in which case the time period must start again. But if the owner of the servient tenement does not stop the owner of the dominant tenement from using the easement during the 20-year period, the owner of the dominant tenement has the right to use the easement forever.

In Figure 4.3, assume that Erin owns lot A and Jeffrey owns lot B. Lots A, B, C, and D are very large lots. Jeffrey works at a school that is near the corner of lots A and C. As you can see, it will be easier and faster for Jeffrey to get to work if he cuts across lot A. If Jeffrey starts to use this shortcut, and does so regularly for 20 years, Jeffrey will acquire an easement interest in Erin's property, by prescription. If Erin wants to stop this from happening, all she has to do is tell Jeffrey to stop using her land at any time during the 20-year period. Afterward, it will be too late to prevent Jeffrey from acquiring an easement interest in her land. If, after 12 years of using the shortcut, Jeffrey sells lot B to Jake, and Jake continues to use the shortcut, the 20-year period continues to run, and Jake will be able to claim an easement interest in Erin's land, by prescription, after eight more years of using the shortcut.

Encroachment by Prescription

If an owner of land permits an encroachment to exist for at least 20 years, the right to object to the encroachment is lost and the landowner can no longer demand its removal. For example, if Adam's shed is partially situated on Keith's property and the shed has been there for at least 20 years, Adam will not have to remove it. This is known as **encroachment by prescription**.

Title to Land

In real estate law, **title** is another word for ownership. A person who holds the fee simple estate in a property is said to have *title* to that property. He or she is known as the owner of the property.

Property can be owned by one person alone or by two or more people together. When two or more people own property together, they can hold title together either as **joint tenants** or as **tenants-in-common**.

encroachment by prescription
the right to keep an encroaching building or structure on land after it has remained there for 20 years

title
the legal right to the ownership and possession of property; evidence of such a right

joint tenants
two or more people in an ownership arrangement whereby, on the death of one owner, the survivor(s) inherits the deceased's share

tenants-in-common
two or more people in an ownership arrangement whereby, on the death of one owner, the deceased's share passes to his or her heirs rather than to the other owners; no right of survivorship

Figure 4.3   A Non-Mutual Easement

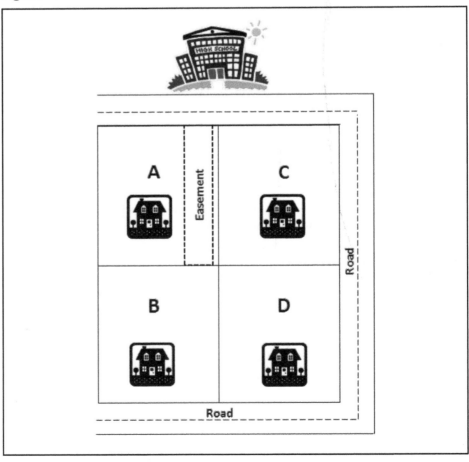

Joint Tenants

When two or more people hold title to property as joint tenants, each person has an undivided interest in the entire property, as opposed to an actual percentage of ownership. For example, if Carla and Daniel own a property as joint tenants, they together own 100 percent of the property. The most significant feature of this type of ownership is the **right of survivorship** among the joint tenants. When one joint tenant dies, his or her interest automatically **vests** in the surviving joint tenant or tenants—in other words, the surviving joint tenant or tenants automatically receive the deceased's interest.

Because of the right of survivorship, a person holding title as a joint tenant cannot grant his or her interest in the property by will. Let's return to the Carla–Daniel example. Because there is a joint tenancy, Carla's interest automatically vests in Daniel upon Carla's death. If Carla has made a will that leaves her interest in the property to Raymond, Raymond will not inherit the property when Carla dies; such a provision in a will would have no effect. As mentioned above, a joint tenancy can be between more than two people. For example, assume that Bob, Brian, and Brenda own a property as joint tenants. If Bob dies, his interest automatically vests in Brian and Brenda, as joint tenants, who now each have a one-half interest in the property. If Brian then dies, his interest vests in Brenda, who becomes the sole owner of the property.

A joint tenancy can be unilaterally severed by a joint tenant without the consent, or even the knowledge, of the other joint tenant(s). To sever a joint tenancy, all a joint tenant has to do is transfer his or her interest in the property to him/herself. He or she will now own the property as a tenant-in-common with the other owner(s). (Tenants-in-common are discussed below.)

Married couples who own property usually hold title as joint tenants. A wife will likely want her husband to inherit her property when she dies, and vice versa. Therefore, the right of survivorship will save time and money when one of them dies. Because the property will automatically go to the surviving spouse, probate fees are minimized and administering the deceased's estate is easier. (Probate fees and estates are discussed in Chapter 8.)

right of survivorship
automatic vesting of an interest in the surviving joint tenant or tenants when one joint tenant dies

vests
provides an immediate right to present or future ownership or possession

Tenants-in-Common

When two or more people hold title as tenants-in-common there is no right of survivorship and the interests do not have to be equal. For example, one tenant-in-common can own three-quarters of the property while the other tenant-in-common owns one-quarter. While each tenant-in-common may not be equal, each tenant still has an undivided interest in the entire property (as opposed to an exclusive right to part of the property). Each tenant-in-common may transfer his or her individual interest in the property to a third party or dispose of it by will.

For example, assume that Bob and Brian own a property as tenants-in-common. If their interests are equal, then each will have a 50 percent interest in the property. Alternatively, Bob may have a 75 percent interest and Brian only 25 percent. If Bob dies, his interest in the property becomes part of his estate and passes to his heirs by will or intestacy. If Bob sells his interest to David, then Brian and David will own the property as tenants-in-common.

Land Registration Systems

legal description
a description of land that is used in documents creating an interest in land; describes the land with reference to recorded maps, surveys, or plans

Legal documents dealing with real property describe the property by using a **legal description**. For example, if you purchase a home on a corner lot on Madison Avenue, the property will not be described by its municipal address. It will instead be described with reference to recorded maps, surveys, or plans of the land. Most legal descriptions today refer to the land's location within a **registered plan of subdivision**, and they consist of a lot number and a plan number. For example, assume the corner lot on Madison Avenue is part of a large subdivision. When the builder developed the land, he or she would have been required to register a plan showing all the lots created within that subdivision. If the registration number of the plan is 3213 and the corner lot is identified as lot 10, the legal description is Lot 10, Plan 3213. The city or town will come after the lot and plan in the legal description—for example, Lot 10, Plan 3213, Town of Newkirk.

registered plan of subdivision
a plan that is registered on title illustrating the measurements and boundaries of all lots and streets created by the division of a large parcel of land into many smaller lots

The legal description of some properties may involve a **metes and bounds description**, or a **reference plan**, and not a plan of subdivision. These types of legal descriptions are complicated and are beyond the scope of this book.

metes and bounds description
a written description of the boundaries and dimensions of a parcel of land

Documents creating an interest in land and other title-related information are recorded in a land registration system. This system provides deemed notice to the public of any registered interest in land. This means that everyone is deemed (that is, the law treats or considers everyone as knowing) to "know" that a registered interest exists and affects the landowner's title, regardless of whether someone has actual knowledge of this interest. A land registration system also establishes priority between two competing interests in land. For example, assume that Mr. Zimms arranges two mortgages on his property, one with Bank A and the other with Bank B, and he registers both mortgages. The mortgage that is registered first has priority. (The significance of priority is discussed in Chapter 5.) Also, everyone is deemed to know about the existence of these mortgages. Registration of a document constitutes, legally speaking, actual "knowledge."

reference plan
a registered plan that illustrates the boundaries of a parcel of land

There are two land registration systems in Ontario—the Registry System and the Land Titles System. All land in Ontario has already been assigned to one of these two systems.

Registry System

deed
a document that transfers ownership of land

grant
a document that transfers ownership of land

The Registry System was the first land registration system in Ontario. It was established in 1795 and is governed by the *Registry Act*.[1] Under this system, all documents affecting land—for example, **deeds** or **grants**, mortgages, powers of attorney, and subdivision agreements—were recorded in a book called an **abstract book**. The

abstract book
a book in the Registry System that records registered interests in land

---

1   RSO 1990, c. R.20.

actual documents were filed in the registry office and were available for public viewing either in their original paper form or on microfilm. In the Registry System, registration simply provides notice that a document has been registered—it does not guarantee that the document is legally valid or effective. A title search is the only way to determine whether documents registered in the Registry System have the legal effect they claim to have. Title searching is discussed below. The Registry System will soon be eliminated. Eventually all the land in Ontario will be registered in only one system—the Land Titles System.

Land Titles System

The Land Titles System is the second system of land registration. It was established in 1885 and is governed by the *Land Titles Act*.[2] Unlike the Registry System, which simply provides a record of documents affecting title, the Land Titles system provides a statement of title as a fact. In other words, the government guarantees the accuracy of title to land if it is registered in the Land Titles System. Documents affecting land are recorded in a book called the **parcel register**. The parcel register is updated each time a document is registered and therefore always reflects only the current state of title. Under the Land Titles System, the actual documents related to land titles are stored in a computer index and are available for public viewing on microfiche. Ontario is currently in the process of converting all Registry System properties into the Land Titles System.

parcel register
the book in the Land Titles System that records all registered interests in land

Electronic Registration

In ~~1985,~~ Ontario began a major reform to the land registration systems with a project called the Province of Ontario Land Registration Information System (POLARIS). The *Land Registration Reform Act*[3] authorized the implementation of POLARIS's initiatives, including the following:

- automating (computerizing) Ontario's land registration system (title records for all property will be computerized),
- standardizing all title-related forms and procedures,
- converting Registry System properties to the Land Titles System,
- providing for electronic title and execution searching (discussed below),
- providing for electronic registration of documents, and
- converting all paper documents to microfilm.

All property in Ontario has been, or will be, assigned a unique nine-digit number called a **property identifier number (PIN)**, with title information indexed according to this PIN and available electronically. Property continues to be provided with a

property identifier number (PIN)
a unique nine-digit number for each property; used to gain access to the automated title index

---

2 RSO 1990, c. L.5.

3 RSO 1990, c. L.4.

automated title index
a computerized printout listing all documents registered on title

legal description. To obtain the **automated title index** (which shows all title-related information), however, you must use the PIN. Once POLARIS is fully implemented, all property will be in the Land Titles System, and it will be a fully electronic and paperless registration system. Electronic registration (known as e-reg) makes it possible for all documents to be created, signed, exchanged between law offices, maintained, and registered in an electronic format. The software required to use the electronic registration system is called Teraview.[4] Real estate closings can now be conducted electronically from the lawyers' offices as opposed to in person at the land registration offices. This makes the process of completing a real estate closing much simpler and more efficient.

Title Searching

Overview

search the title
conduct an investigation into the status and history of title to land

encumbrances
charges, claims, liens, or liabilities that affect title to a property

It is necessary to **search the title** to a particular piece of land to find out who owns the property and whether that person's ownership interest is subject to any claims or **encumbrances**. Searching title involves checking the entries recorded in the abstract book, the parcel register, and/or the automated title index for a particular piece of land, and then examining the listed documents. Real estate transactions most often give rise to title searches. It is the role of the buyer's real estate lawyer to ensure that the buyer receives the title that was promised by the vendor. The lawyer does this by searching the title to the property. Lawyers do this for two reasons:

1. to confirm that the seller, in fact, owns the property; and
2. to find out what encumbrances are, in fact, outstanding.

If the title search discloses any encumbrances that the seller did not disclose in the agreement of purchase and sale, the buyer's lawyer will ask the seller's lawyer to remove those encumbrances before closing.

When the deal closes, the buyer's lawyer must provide the buyer with an opinion about the state of title. The title search provides the basis upon which the lawyer determines the state of title and provides this opinion. Before conducting a title search, you must determine whether the property is registered in the Registry System or the Land Titles System. Although most Registry System properties have been moved to the Land Titles System, there are still some that have not been converted. The title records will likely now be automated. This means that you will need the PIN to access title-related information in both a Registry System title search and a Land Titles System title search.

---

4 Teraview was developed by Teranet Inc.

Registry System Title Search

A Registry System title search is complicated because you must examine all registered documents affecting title to ensure their legal effectiveness. As discussed above, the Registry System is a notice system only. In other words, it provides notice of the documents registered against title but it does not guarantee the legal effectiveness of any of those documents—nor does it certify the current owner's title. A Registry System title search involves examining the history of ownership of the property for the 40 years prior to the date on which the title search is conducted. For example, if the search is conducted on September 1, 2013, the search will go back to September 1, 1973. To determine who owned the property at the start of the 40-year search period (in this case September 1, 1973), you must find the deed or transfer registered immediately before September 1, 1973. This is usually treated as the **root deed** or **root of title** in a Registry System title search. To conduct the title search, you must obtain a copy of all the documents registered on title during the 40-year search period and examine each document to ensure that all of them are legally valid and effective. This is how you determine good title. The process is based on the premise that a claim against the property that has not been raised for 40 years is no longer a valid claim against the property.

root deed (root of title) the first conveyance of the fee simple estate (a deed, grant, or transfer) registered before the commencement date of a title search

Land Titles System Title Search

In the Land Titles System, the state of title is guaranteed. Therefore, there is no need to conduct a search of title covering the last 40 years. If the parcel register or automated title index reveals Demetre Papsolis to be the owner, then it is guaranteed that he is the legal owner and has good title to the property, subject to any encumbrances that are revealed on the parcel register. Note that title search requirements may differ depending on whether the property was always registered in the Land Titles System or was converted from the Registry System as a result of POLARIS.

Planning Act Search

If the property you are searching is not a whole lot on a plan of subdivision (for example, if it is a part of a lot on a subdivision plan or is on a concession lot), you must also conduct a search called a *Planning Act*[5] search, to determine whether, at any time during the period being searched, the same person who owned the property being searched also owned any adjoining property. The legal implications of such ownership can be serious and must be addressed. The *Planning Act* provides that a landowner is not permitted to sever (divide) his or her land except under certain circumstances. If the owner has not complied with the *Planning Act* in this regard, the would-be buyer will not get valid title to the land. The *Planning Act* applies to properties registered in both the Registry System and the Land Titles System. (*Planning Act* issues are very complicated and are outside the scope of this book.)

---

5 RSO 1990, c. P.13.

Execution Search (Writs of Execution)

execution
the short name for a
writ of execution

writ of execution
a judicial order addressed
to the sheriff requiring the
enforcement of a judgment

An **execution** (short for **writ of execution**) is a claim against a person resulting from a court judgment. That claim is then registered against that person's name with the sheriff of the judicial district in which the person (that is, the debtor) owns real property. Executions create a lien against any lands already owned by the person named in the execution at the time of filing and any lands that the person acquires after the date of filing. If you are buying property, you must make sure that there are no outstanding executions against the owner of the property you are buying.

In the Registry System, you must search executions against everyone who owned the property within the 40-year search period. If there is an execution against either the current owner or any past owner that was registered during or prior to their ownership, it will affect title to the land. For example, if Brittania owned the property from 1987 to 1998, and an execution was registered against her in 1992, it will affect title. Similarly, if the execution was registered in 1985, it will affect title because she took title after the execution was registered. If, however, the execution was registered in 2001, it will not have any impact on her title because the execution was filed after she no longer owned the property.

In the Land Titles System, you have to search executions against the current owner only. It should be noted that if the buyer obtains title insurance, executions in the Registry System are treated the same as in the Land Titles System—they are searched only against the current owner. (Title insurance is discussed below.)

Execution searching is fully automated and can therefore be performed online using the Teraview software. Most lawyers who practise real estate law have the Teraview software. The software is also available for the public's use at the land registration offices.

Title Insurance

Title insurance is insurance similar to home insurance or car insurance. With home insurance or car insurance, you purchase a policy and pay a premium to protect yourself in the event that you suffer loss or damage to your home or your car. With title insurance, you purchase a policy (through your lawyer) and pay a premium to protect yourself in the event that you suffer loss or damage as a result of problems with title to real property.

mortgagee
a lender who uses real property as security for a loan

title opinion
a lawyer's statement as
to whether or not title
to a property is good

A title insurance policy can be issued in favour both of purchasers of real property and of **mortgagees** (that is, lenders of money secured by real property). Both have a vested interest in the state of title of the property they are buying or loaning money against. Both want protection in the event title problems arise. In the past, a purchaser's or mortgagee's only option was to rely on the lawyer's legal opinion to confirm that there were no problems with title to the property. While purchasers and mortgagees can still choose to rely on the lawyer's **title opinion** or certification of title, there is also a second option—namely, title insurance. Title insurance has become increasingly prevalent in real estate transactions. In fact, mortgagees often insist on title insurance to ensure that any future problems with title are easily corrected. In this chapter, we focus on title insurance policies issued to purchasers of real property (called an owner's policy), as opposed to those issued to mortgagees, which we discuss in Chapter 5. The two policies are very similar.

An insured owner's policy remains in effect as long as the owner has title to the property. If a problem arises with title—if, for example, it emerges that there are realty taxes that the seller did not pay before closing—the purchaser contacts the insurance company, and the insurance company corrects the problem by paying the taxes owing. The purchaser does not have to sue the lawyer and establish negligence on the lawyer's part, which is what a purchaser has to do if he/she relies on the lawyer's title opinion.

The problem with relying on the lawyer's title opinion is that if certain kinds of problems arise with the title—for example, a fraud by the seller that the lawyer could not be expected to detect—then the purchaser will not have a valid cause of action against the lawyer and will not be compensated. In addition, a purchaser cannot make a claim against the lawyer for a problem that arises from any fraudulent action after the purchase transaction is completed, such as a charge or lien fraudulently registered after completion of the transaction.

For these reasons, title insurance may be the better option for the purchaser. All a purchaser has to do is prove that a problem exists that is covered by the policy purchased, and the purchaser is then covered for damages or the cost of clearing title.

Before providing coverage for a particular title, a title insurer will require the purchaser's lawyer to make certain representations with respect to title and may exclude certain risks that it is not prepared to cover. Unlike other types of insurance, the premium for title insurance is paid only once, with no annual renewals.

In addition to the cost of the policy, the purchaser will have to pay his/her lawyer's legal fees and disbursements for the searches and inquiries required by the title insurance company. Because these searches will be fewer than those required for a lawyer's opinion of title, the cost of disbursements charged to a purchaser who is obtaining title insurance will be correspondingly less. For this reason, obtaining title insurance may be less expensive than choosing to rely on a lawyer's opinion on title.

There is another reason that title insurance is the cheaper option. Most purchasers borrow money from the bank to finance the purchase of real property. The bank requires a survey of the property being purchased to ensure that the structures on it are actually in the proper location. Surveys are expensive and are often lost, or they become outdated owing to the passage of time or to changes in the location of structures on the property. With title insurance, however, a survey is not required. One of the assurances provided by the insurer is that the property complies with the **set-back requirements** of the relevant bylaw. If it doesn't, the insurer will take whatever measures are necessary to correct this problem. Also, when title insurance is obtained, an execution search is conducted against the current owner only, even in the Registry System, and this saves the purchaser a lot of money. As mentioned, the usual practice is to search executions against everyone who owned the property during the 40-year search period. With title insurance, you need to search against only the current owner, as is the practice in the Land Titles System.

set-back requirement
a provision in a bylaw stating the minimum required distance between structures and a lot line

In every real estate transaction, a lawyer must advise his/her client about the two options for assuring good title—(1) the lawyer's certification of title or (2) title insurance. If the client chooses to purchase a title insurance policy, the lawyer applies for it on the purchaser's behalf. Only a lawyer can arrange title insurance.

Lawyers typically arrange title insurance on behalf of a client who is purchasing property. However, lawyers can purchase a title insurance policy for existing property owners as well, who may be concerned about potential fraud. The introduction of title insurance has greatly expedited and simplified real estate transactions in Ontario.

Figure 4.4   Lawyer's Title Opinion Versus Title Insurance: A Comparison

Lawyer's Certification of Title	Title Insurance Policy
Lawyer certifies that purchaser has good title	Lawyer obtains title insurance policy on behalf of purchaser
If there is a title problem, purchaser contacts lawyer • If lawyer can't fix problem, purchaser can sue lawyer for negligence • Purchaser must prove lawyer was negligent	If there is a title problem, purchaser contacts title insurance company • Insurance company will fix problem (as long as it is covered by the policy) • Purchaser is covered for damages or the cost of clearing title
Purchaser can make a claim against lawyer for title problems that arise after closing as a result of lawyer's negligence	Purchaser contacts title insurance company for title problems that arise after closing as a result of lawyer's negligence
Purchaser cannot make a claim against lawyer for title problems that arise after closing as a result of fraud	Purchaser is protected against title problems that arise after closing as a result of fraud

KEY TERMS

abstract book, 58
adverse interest in land, 54
adversely, 54
adverse possession, 54
agreement of purchase and sale, 48
automated title index, 60
bylaws (municipal), 49
chattels, 48
commit waste, 50
deed, 58
doctrine of escheat, 49
dominant tenement, 52
easement, 52
easement by prescription, 55
encroachment, 53
encroachment agreement, 53
encroachment by prescription, 56
encumbrances, 60
escheats, 49
estate, 48

exclusive possession, 49
execution, 62
express grant, 53
expropriate, 49
extinguished, 54
fair market value, 49
fee simple estate, 49
fixtures, 48
forfeit, 48
grant, 58
interests in land, 49
joint tenants, 56
Land Titles System, 54
leasehold estate, 49
legal description, 58
life estate, 49
life tenant, 50
metes and bounds description, 58
mortgagee, 62
parcel register, 59

personal property, 48
prescription, 53
property identifier number (PIN), 59
real property, 48
reference plan, 58
registered plan of subdivision, 58
Registry System, 54
remainderman, 50
restrictive covenant, 54
right of survivorship, 57
right of way, 52
root deed (root of title), 61
search the title, 60
servient tenement, 52
set-back requirement, 63
tenants-in-common, 56
title, 56
title opinion, 62
vests, 57
writ of execution, 62

REVIEW QUESTIONS

1. What does real property include?

2. State whether each of the following is a chattel or a fixture. Explain your answer.

   - desk
   - built-in bookshelf
   - above-ground swimming pool
   - ceiling fan

3. Ari died without leaving a will and without anyone entitled to inherit his property. What will happen to the house he owned?

4. What is the greatest estate in land that a person can have?

5. Sam, a senior, transferred a life estate in his home to Susan, and the fee simple estate to Jonas. Does Jonas have the right to move into the home whenever he wants? Explain your answer.

6. Sam, a senior, transferred a life estate in his home to Susan, and the fee simple estate to Jonas. Susan granted a leasehold estate to Bruno. What happens when Susan dies? Is Jonas required to continue renting to Bruno?

7. Michael and Elliott own a property together as joint tenants. What will happen to the property if Michael dies?

8. If Jake grants Ernie the right to use part of his land, what type of interest does Ernie have in Jake's land?

9. What happens if a person exercises exclusive possession of another person's property, without the owner's permission but openly (with the owner's knowledge) and continuously, for over 10 years?

10. How is land described in a legal document?

11. You are conducting a title search in 2013. The following deeds/transfers are registered on title. Which of the following is most likely to be the root deed? Explain your answer.

    - September 16, 2006
    - June 9, 1992
    - March 18, 1980
    - November 8, 1971
    - April 3, 1960

12. What options are available to a purchaser of property to ensure that he or she will have good title to the property?

Mortgages

5

LEARNING OUTCOMES

After reading this chapter, you should be able to:

- Understand basic mortgage concepts
- Identify the parties to a mortgage
- Understand the different ways a mortgage can be created
- Explain basic mortgage terminology
- Understand the relevant dates in a mortgage
- Explain the obligations of a mortgagor
- Identify the priority of mortgages
- Understand and apply the various mortgage remedies available to a mortgagee

Introduction

An owner of real property—either land alone or land with a building (for example, a house) on it—may want to borrow money and to use the real property as **security** for the loan. This type of loan is called a **mortgage**.

A mortgage is also known as a **charge**. Historically, there was a significant distinction between the terms "mortgage" and "charge." A *mortgage* was the means of securing a loan against land registered in the Registry System; a *charge* was the means of securing a loan against land registered in the Land Titles System. Today, the terms "mortgage" and "charge" mean the same thing and are used interchangeably; there is no legal distinction between them.

A loan that is secured by a mortgage can be granted when a person buys a property or when a person already owns a property. For example, if Alan buys a new house for $300,000 and he has $100,000, he will need to borrow $200,000. The loan he obtains will be secured with a mortgage. If Alan already owns a property—for example, a cottage—and he wants to borrow $35,000 so that he can buy a new car, he can mortgage the cottage to secure the loan. In the second situation, Alan would be **refinancing**, which means that he is borrowing money, using as security property that he already owns rather than (as in the previous example) property that he is buying.

Parties to a Mortgage

The bank, company, or individual who lends money secured by a mortgage is called the **mortgagee** or the **chargee**. As with the terms *mortgage* and *charge*, the terms *mortgagee* and *chargee* are used interchangeably. The landowner who borrows money is called the **mortgagor** or **chargor**. For example, if Alan borrows $50,000 from ABC Bank, and the loan is secured by a mortgage on Alan's home, Alan is the mortgagor or chargor, and ABC Bank is the mortgagee or chargee.

For the remainder of this chapter, when discussing charges and mortgages, we use the terms *mortgagor* and *chargor*, and *mortgage* and *charge* interchangeably, as we do *mortgagee* and *chargee*. In addition, we sometimes refer to the mortgagor/chargor as the borrower, and the mortgagee/chargee as the lender. It is common to hear all these terms being used when arranging a mortgage.

The mortgagor can be an individual or a corporation. For example, if Alan's company, Alan's Dental Supplies Inc., is the owner of Alan's home, the mortgagor is Alan's Dental Supplies Inc. The mortgagee can be either an **institutional lender** or a **private lender**. An institutional lender is a bank, trust company, insurance company, or credit union that is in the business of lending money. A private lender is a lender that is not a lending institution, and can be a person or a business.

When people need to borrow money, they tend to go to a lending institution rather than to a private lender. Private lenders usually charge higher fees and a higher **interest rate**. A mortgagor typically goes to a private lender when an institution will not lend the money because the loan might be too risky.

security
what the lender/chargee/mortgagee receives in exchange for lending money

mortgage/charge
a loan that is secured by real property

refinance
obtain a mortgage on property currently owned

mortgagee/chargee
the lender in a mortgage transaction

mortgagor/chargor
the borrower in a mortgage transaction

institutional lender
a bank, trust company, credit union, or insurance company that is in the business of lending money

private lender
an individual or business that lends money but is not a bank, trust company, credit union, or insurance company

interest rate
the percentage of interest, on an annual basis, that the mortgagee charges the mortgagor on the principal amount of money borrowed under a loan

If there are multiple borrowers, their liability to the lender is known as *joint and several liability*.[1] This means that the liability of each borrower is not limited to his/her/its share or interest in the property. Each borrower is liable for the full amount of the debt. Therefore, when a mortgage is in default, the lender can go after each borrower to the extent the lender is able to collect from each. While lenders cannot collect more than the amount that is owed to them, they can choose to collect the entire debt from only one of the borrowers, if that would be easier or advantageous for them.

Mortgage Payments

The amount of money borrowed by the mortgagor (or loaned by the mortgagee) is called the **principal**. It is repaid over time, together with **interest**—that is, an amount added to the loan for the right to obtain and use the money advanced. Interest provides an incentive to banks and other lenders to lend money; it allows them to earn money on the amount loaned.

One of the main factors determining how much interest is payable under a mortgage is the interest rate, which is calculated as an annual percentage of the amount of the loan. A mortgage can have a **fixed interest rate** or a **variable interest rate**.

A fixed interest rate means that the interest rate will not fluctuate during the term of the charge. For example, if a charge has a fixed interest rate of 5 percent, this rate will remain constant for the entire term of the charge. A variable interest rate means that the interest rate will fluctuate during the term of the charge in accordance with the **prime lending rate**, as set by the Bank of Canada. A variable rate will typically be expressed as "prime plus ___" percent. In this way, the interest rate fluctuates with changing market conditions. As the prime lending rate goes up and down, so does the interest rate on the charge.

Another factor that determines how much interest is payable under a mortgage is the frequency with which interest is calculated. The more frequently interest is calculated, the more interest the mortgagor ends up paying. The frequency of calculation is the frequency with which the interest is compounded. For example, a monthly calculation or compounding period (12 times per year) will work out to more interest than an annual compounding period (once per year). For this reason, you need to pay attention to more than just the rate of interest in a charge. A lower rate of interest can be offset by greater frequency of calculation. Most of the time, interest is calculated semi-annually, which is twice per year.

Principal and interest payable under a charge are paid in arrears—in other words, at the end of a period—and not in advance. If the loan money is given to the chargor on the first of the month, charge payments are not due until the first of the following

principal
the amount of money borrowed

interest
the amount, added to the principal amount of a loan, that the mortgagor must pay in return for the right to obtain and use the money advanced

fixed interest rate
a rate of interest that remains the same for the term of the charge

variable interest rate
a rate of interest that fluctuates with changing market conditions during the term of the charge

prime lending rate
the interest rate charged by banks to their largest, most secure, and most creditworthy customers on short-term loans

---

1 *Mortgages Act*, RSO 1990, c. M.40, s. 8.

month. The interest paid at that time is for the use of the money during the preceding month. This contrasts with residential rental payments, which are usually payable on the first of each month for the use of the rented premises for that month. In most cases, mortgage payments are made monthly but can be made at different intervals as well, such as weekly or biweekly. For the rest of the chapter, we assume that mortgage payments are made monthly.

How a Mortgage Is Created

equity
the net value of property after the value of the encumbrances is deducted

As mentioned above, a property owner may refinance its/his/her property in order to take out **equity**. For example, if Sam owns a property without a mortgage and wants to borrow $100,000, he can go to the bank to arrange a mortgage. If Sam has an existing mortgage with the bank in the amount of $50,000 but wants to increase the amount to $100,000 he can go to the bank to arrange a mortgage for the higher amount. This is referred to as a new mortgage. A purchaser of real property can pay the entire purchase price in cash if he or she has enough money to do so. However, most of the time, a purchaser needs to borrow money to be able to complete the purchase of real property. A purchaser can therefore

- arrange his/her own new mortgage (*new mortgage*),
- assume an existing mortgage registered on title and pay the vendor the purchase price less the amount of this mortgage (*assumed mortgage*), or
- borrow money from the vendor and give the vendor a mortgage on the property (*vendor take-back mortgage*).

These are the most common types of mortgages or charges that arise in the typical purchase and sale transaction. Usually a purchaser will require only one mortgage. However, if they need them, purchasers can have more than one mortgage. For example, a purchaser can assume an existing mortgage and also arrange a new one, or a purchaser can arrange two new mortgages.

New Mortgage (Arranged Mortgage)

A new mortgage is used when an owner or purchaser of real property goes to a lender—for example, a bank—and arranges to borrow money. The bank will provide mortgage instructions to the purchaser's lawyer. The lawyer will assure the bank's security for the loan by preparing and registering a mortgage against title to the property and then use the money for the transaction.

For example, assume that Sam is selling his home for $300,000. Bob wants to buy the home but only has $200,000. Bob can borrow the additional funds he needs from the bank and use the home as security for the loan. The bank will give Bob $100,000 (through Bob's lawyer) and Bob will give the bank a charge on the home. Bob can now give Sam the $300,000, and Sam will transfer title to Bob. Title to the real property will show Bob as the owner and a charge in favour of the bank in the amount of $100,000. See Figure 5.1.

Figure 5.1   New Mortgage

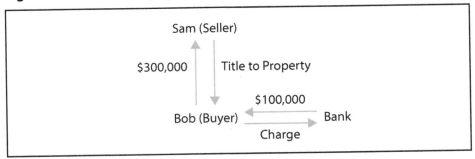

Assumed Mortgage

If a purchaser of real property wants to take over an existing mortgage on the property he/she is buying, the purchaser is said to be **assuming the mortgage**.

A purchaser may agree to assume an existing mortgage registered against title to the property he or she is buying when the existing mortgage has favourable terms. In this situation, the purchaser will pay the vendor the purchase price, less the amount of the outstanding mortgage.

For example, suppose Sam is selling his home to Bob for $300,000, and there is an outstanding charge in favour of Friendly Bank in the amount of $100,000. Bob will pay Sam $200,000 and assume the charge in favour of Friendly Bank.

As Figure 5.2 shows, Sam owed Friendly Bank $100,000. Bob will assume this charge and pay Sam the difference—that is, $200,000. Bob will replace Sam in the relationship with Friendly Bank and assume all existing charge-related obligations. Before assuming the charge, Bob will need Friendly Bank's consent.

It makes sense for a purchaser to assume an existing mortgage when the interest rate on the mortgage is lower than it would be if the purchaser were arranging a new mortgage. For example, if the interest rate on Sam's mortgage is 3 percent, and the best interest rate that Bob can obtain from the bank is 5 percent, then Bob is better off assuming Sam's mortgage. Sam also benefits from his mortgage being assumed.

assuming a mortgage
taking over an existing mortgage

Figure 5.2   Assumed Mortgage

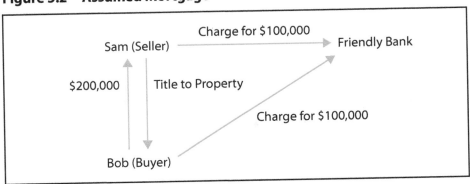

If a mortgagor pays the amount owing on a mortgage before the end of the agreed-upon time for doing so (that is, the term), the lender will likely charge a **prepayment penalty** for breaking the contract early. But if Bob assumes Sam's mortgage, Sam will not be breaking the contract in this way and will not have to pay the penalty.

Vendor Take-Back Mortgage

Sometimes a purchaser is unable to raise enough money to purchase the property. For example, if the purchaser has a bad credit history or does not have enough income, the purchaser will be unable to borrow money from a bank or another lender. In this situation, a purchaser may ask the vendor to lend the purchaser money. If the vendor wants the deal to close, he/she can advance the funds needed to the purchaser, and take back a charge on the property. This is called a **vendor take-back mortgage**.

For example, assume that Sam is selling a property for $300,000 and wants to complete the deal with Bob, an interested buyer. Bob only has $200,000 and also wants to complete the deal. Sam can accept the $200,000 and effectively loan Bob the difference by taking back a charge on the property in the amount of $100,000. See Figure 5.3.

A vendor take-back mortgage may also be negotiated between a purchaser and a vendor when the purchaser is able to get a mortgage from a lender, such as a bank, but is unable to get enough money. For example, if Bob is able to borrow only $60,000 from the bank, Bob may ask Sam to take back a charge in the amount of $40,000 so that Bob is able to complete the transaction. In this example, Bob would have a first mortgage with the bank and a second mortgage with Sam.

Figure 5.3   Vendor Take-Back Mortgage

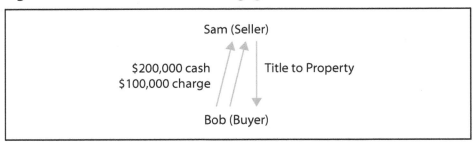

Factors to Consider When Lending Money

When deciding whether or not to lend money secured by real property, the lender will look at two main factors: equity and the **covenant**. These factors determine how risky the loan will be for the lender.

Equity is the value of the property, less the amount of mortgages registered against title. For example, if a property is worth $350,000, and there is a mortgage with an outstanding balance of $200,000 registered on title, the equity in the property is

---

prepayment penalty
an amount that a borrower may have to pay when ending a mortgage contract earlier than the balance due date

vendor take-back mortgage
a charge created when the seller agrees to lend the buyer money toward the purchase price of the property, and the buyer gives the seller a charge on the property as security for the loan

covenant
a personal promise to pay

$150,000. This value is important because the lender must be confident that if the borrower defaults on the mortgage, the money that is invested in the mortgage is safe. In other words, if the property is sold under power of sale (discussed later in this chapter), the mortgagee will likely not lose any money because there is a lot of equity in the property. This makes the mortgagee's investment a safe one.

A *covenant* is the borrower's promise to pay back the money. A covenant is stronger when the borrower has a high income and good credit.

The importance of these two factors depends on the lender. For example, institutional lenders place a high importance on the covenant. Private lenders, on the other hand, may be more concerned about the equity.

Mortgage Terminology

Term and Amortization

The **term** of the mortgage is the length of time covered by the contract between the mortgagee and the mortgagor. A term is usually between one and five years. For example, assume Alan borrows money from Friendly Bank on December 1, 2013. If the mortgage is for a two-year term, the mortgage contract between Alan and Friendly Bank will end on December 1, 2015.

The **amortization period** is the length of time that it will take to pay off a mortgage in full by means of a constant **blended payment** of principal and interest. (Blended payments are discussed below.) A typical amortization period is 25 years; if it is shorter, the payments will be larger and the mortgage will therefore be paid off sooner. An amortization schedule sets out how blended payments are applied each month. It shows what part of each monthly payment is applied toward principal and what part is applied toward interest.

Figure 5.4 is an amortization schedule for a charge of $100,000 that has a fixed interest rate of 5 percent, a 2-year term, and a 25-year amortization period. As you can see, with each monthly payment, the amount applied to the principal of the mortgage increases and the amount applied to the interest decreases. After 24 months of making blended payments, the amount still owing on the mortgage is $95,740.20. This amount is called a **balloon payment**. The borrower can either pay this amount in full (if he or she has the money), renew the term of the charge at the current interest rate, or refinance with a different lender. Renewing the term of the mortgage and/or refinancing the amount outstanding requires the mortgagor to negotiate with the existing mortgagee or a different mortgagee to obtain the best interest rate possible.

For example, let's assume that Alan does not have the $95,740.20 he needs to pay off the mortgage. Alan may ask Friendly Bank what interest rate it can offer him and, if he is happy with that rate, he can renew the mortgage for another term. If, however, Alan can get a better rate at Data Bank of Canada, he may decide to arrange a new mortgage with that bank. If he chooses this option, he will use the money he obtains from Data Bank of Canada to pay off the amount outstanding on his mortgage with Friendly Bank.

term
the length of time that the borrower and lender are bound by the mortgage contract

amortization period
the length of time it takes to repay a loan in full if the schedule of monthly payments in the charge is followed

blended payment
a charge payment combining principal and interest into regular equal monthly payments

balloon payment
the final payment for the amount of principal that remains unpaid at the end of the term of a charge

Figure 5.4 Amortization Schedule—Principal $100,000, Interest 5%, 2-Year Term, 25-Year Amortization

# of Payment	Principal Outstanding	Payment	Interest Portion	Principal Portion	Principal Balance After Payment
1	$100,000.00	$581.61	$412.39	$169.22	$99,830.78
2	$99,830.78	$581.61	$411.69	$169.92	$99,660.87
3	$99,660.87	$581.61	$410.99	$170.62	$99,490.25
4	$99,490.25	$581.61	$410.29	$171.32	$99,318.93
5	$99,318.93	$581.61	$409.58	$172.03	$99,146.90
6	$99,146.90	$581.61	$408.87	$172.74	$98,974.16
7	$98,974.16	$581.61	$408.16	$173.45	$98,800.72
8	$98,800.72	$581.61	$407.45	$174.16	$98,626.55
9	$98,626.55	$581.61	$406.73	$174.88	$98,451.67
10	$98,451.67	$581.61	$406.01	$175.60	$98,276.06
11	$98,276.06	$581.61	$405.28	$176.33	$98,099.74
12	$98,099.74	$581.61	$404.56	$177.06	$97,922.68
13	$97,922.68	$581.61	$403.82	$177.79	$97,744.90
14	$97,744.90	$581.61	$403.09	$178.52	$97,566.38
15	$97,566.38	$581.61	$402.36	$179.25	$97,387.12
16	$97,387.12	$581.61	$401.62	$179.99	$97,207.13
17	$97,207.13	$581.61	$400.87	$180.74	$97,026.39
18	$97,026.39	$581.61	$400.13	$181.48	$96,844.91
19	$96,844.91	$581.61	$399.38	$182.23	$96,662.68
20	$96,662.68	$581.61	$398.63	$182.98	$96,479.70
21	$96,479.70	$581.61	$397.87	$183.74	$96,295.97
22	$96,295.97	$581.61	$397.12	$184.49	$96,111.47
23	$96,111.47	$581.61	$396.36	$185.25	$95,926.22
24	$95,926.22	$581.61	$395.59	$186.02	$95,740.20

Blended and Non-Blended Payments

Blended payments, also known as amortized payments, blend or combine principal and interest into one single monthly payment. Although the payment amount remains the same each month, part of each payment is applied toward principal and part is applied toward interest. Initially, a greater portion of each monthly payment is applied toward interest, rather than principal. Gradually, throughout the term of the loan, more is applied toward principal and less toward interest.

As you can see in Figure 5.4's amortization schedule, the monthly payment of $581.61 combines principal and interest. This schedule also shows that, initially, a greater portion of each monthly payment is applied toward interest than to principal. Gradually, as the term of the loan proceeds, more will be applied toward principal and less toward interest. In the 24th payment, for example, $395.59 is applied to interest and $186.02 is applied to principal.

A **non-blended payment** does not blend principal and interest. In this case, the amount of principal and the amount of interest in each payment are separate and distinct. The mortgagor may pay interest only, or may pay interest plus a fixed amount of principal. For example (to return to the example used above), if Alan pays interest only on the loan of $100,000, his monthly payment will be approximately $416.66, and it would cover only the amount owing for interest. At the end of the term, Alan will still owe the principal amount of the loan—$100,000.

A non-blended payment could also be a separate payment of interest together with a fixed amount of principal. The amount of principal repaid each month is a fixed amount, to which is added a separate interest payment, calculated as a percentage of the outstanding principal. The amount of interest payable each month varies, depending on the outstanding principal. If Alan, for example, pays $100 toward principal each month, plus interest, his outstanding balance of principal will decrease each month by $100. As a result, the amount of interest payable will also decrease each month, as less principal remains owing.

Non-blended payments are more common with private lenders. Institutional lenders almost always require blended payments.

> **non-blended payment**
> a charge payment that does not blend or combine principal and interest into equal payments; the amount of principal (if any) repaid each month is a fixed amount and the calculation of interest is based on the outstanding principal at the time

Open and Closed Mortgages

An **open mortgage** is a mortgage that permits the mortgagor to pay off the principal, or any portion of the principal, whenever he or she wants to. For example, assume Alan has an open mortgage with ABC Bank and there are two years left on his five-year term. If Alan receives a $10,000 bonus from work, he can use this money to pay down his mortgage, without having to pay a penalty. Similarly, if Alan inherits $100,000, he can use this money to pay off his mortgage in full, without paying a penalty for prepaying the mortgage before the end of the term.

If, on the other hand, Alan's mortgage is a **closed mortgage**, the bank can refuse early repayment. The bank might refuse early repayment because it does not want to lose the additional amount of interest that it will receive during the last two years of the loan. In this situation, the bank will permit early repayment provided that Alan pays an additional amount as a penalty, to compensate the bank for the interest

> **open mortgage**
> a mortgage that permits repayment of the loan before the expiry of the term

> **closed mortgage**
> a mortgage that prohibits repayment of the loan (unless a penalty is paid) before the expiry of the term

that it is losing by the loan's ending before its expected duration. This means that if Alan wants to use his $10,000 bonus to pay down his mortgage, he will pay a penalty on the $10,000. If he wants to use his inheritance to pay off the entire mortgage, he will pay a penalty on the entire $100,000.

Closed mortgages typically have a lower interest rate and are for a longer term. A mortgagee is prepared to offer a lower interest rate for a closed mortgage because interest payments will continue for the duration of the term of the mortgage. If a mortgage is open, the mortgagor will pay a higher interest rate in exchange for the right to pay off part or all of the mortgage at any time before the end of the term. Most closed mortgages have privilege(s) included in the mortgage that allow a mortgagor to pay off some of the principal at specific times. These privileges are called *open privileges*. A closed mortgage that contains open privilege(s) is known as a **partially open mortgage**. For example, an open privilege might allow the mortgagor to pay off up to 15 percent of the principal on the anniversary date of the mortgage for each year of the term. Different lenders have different open privileges. This is something that a mortgagor can shop around for and negotiate before arranging a charge. See Figure 5.5.

partially open mortgage
a closed mortgage with some repayment provisions

Figure 5.5 Arranging a New Mortgage: Considerations

Principal amount	Amount of money being borrowed.
Interest rate (and frequency of calculation)	Both affect how much the loan will cost the borrower.
Prepayment privileges	Can the borrower pay off any portion of the principal prior to maturity? Open Mortgage—borrower can pay off all or part of the principal, at any time, with no penalty Closed Mortgage—borrower cannot pay off any part of the principal—must pay a penalty if prepayment occurs Partially Open Mortgage—borrower can pay off only a specified amount of the principal, at specified times, with no penalty
Term	How long will the borrower and lender be bound by the mortgage contract?
Payment provisions	Are the mortgage payments blended or non-blended? Blended—payment combines principal and interest into equal monthly payments Non-blended—payment does not combine principal and interest into equal payments; amount of principal repaid each month is a fixed amount and the amount of interest is calculated on the outstanding balance at the time
Payment date	Will mortgage payments be made on the first of the month?
Payment frequency	Will payments be made monthly, weekly, biweekly?

Standard Charge Terms

When a borrower signs a mortgage, he or she is also bound by the mortgagee's **standard charge terms**. Standard charge terms set out in detail the obligations of the mortgagor and the rights of the mortgagee. It is important that, before signing the mortgage, a borrower clearly understand his or her obligations to the lender and the consequences of breaching those obligations. The obligation to make regular mortgage payments is an obvious obligation, but other obligations listed in the standard charge terms may be less obvious. The obligations of a mortgagor, discussed below, include the obligations to

- make payments to prior mortgagees,
- make payments for realty taxes,
- maintain the property, and
- insure the property against loss or damage by fire.

The borrower is given a copy of the standard charge terms before signing the mortgage. The borrower's lawyer has an obligation to explain the standard charge terms to the borrower and then to have the borrower acknowledge, in writing, that he or she has received a copy of them. Once the mortgagor acknowledges receiving a copy of the standard charge terms, he or she is bound by them.

Most institutional lenders have their own preprinted set of standard charge terms which they either forward to the borrower's lawyer or make available online. Although one lender's version may be slightly different from another's, the contents of all lenders' standard charge terms are virtually the same. A generic form of standard charge terms is easily available for lenders who do not have their own preprinted set.

> **standard charge terms**
> mortgage terms setting out the obligations of the mortgagor and the rights of the mortgagee; used in all mortgages issued by an institutional lender

Relevant Dates

The mortgage starts on the date that the money is given to the borrower (through the borrower's lawyer). Interest is calculated from this date, which is known as the **interest adjustment date (IAD)**. The first mortgage payment will be made one month later because, as noted above, mortgage payments are paid in arrears (that is, at the end of a period), and not in advance. For example, assume Julie arranges a mortgage and the bank gives her the money on October 1, 2013. The interest adjustment date is October 1, 2013, and the first regular payment will be due on November 1, 2013. Subsequent monthly payments are due on the first of each month. If the mortgage is for a two-year term, the mortgage will come due two years after it started, which will be on October 1, 2015. This is the date that the term ends and is called the **balance due date**.

If a mortgage does not start on the first of the month, the interest adjustment date is the date the funds are advanced, and the first payment date will be a month later. For example, if a mortgage with a five-year term starts on October 5, 2013, the interest adjustment date is October 5, 2013; the first payment date is November 5, 2013; and the balance due date is October 5, 2018. Sometimes the mortgagee wants the

> **interest adjustment date (IAD)**
> the date on which an adjustment is made for interest that accumulates between the date the loan was advanced and the charge payment date for the following month; assuming charge payments are made monthly, this date will be one month before the date of the first regular payment

> **balance due date**
> the date that the term of a mortgage ends

monthly mortgage payments to be paid on the first day of each month, regardless of what day of the month the money was advanced. For example, assume that Charles borrows money on March 5 and arranges for monthly payments on the first of each month. April 1 will be the interest adjustment date. Thereafter, payments will be made on the first of each month, and the loan is treated as if advanced on the first of the month. When—as in this example—the loan is advanced on a date different than the payment date, an adjustment needs to be made for interest accrued between the date the loan was advanced (March 5) and the interest adjustment date (April 1).

Mortgage Priorities

priority
the interest of a mortgagee that is in preference to another mortgagee

After a mortgage is arranged, it must be registered on title. The time and date of registration will determine the mortgage's **priority**. This is important only when there is more than one mortgage registered on title. The mortgage with the earlier registration date will have priority, regardless of the date the mortgage was arranged. In the event of default, the mortgage with priority will be paid out first.

For example, assume Len has a mortgage with Friendly Bank that was arranged on March 1 and registered on March 3, and a mortgage with Data Bank of Canada that was arranged on March 2 and registered on March 2. Because it was registered first, the mortgage with Data Bank of Canada has priority, even though it was arranged after the Friendly Bank mortgage. The mortgage with Data Bank of Canada is a first mortgage and the mortgage with Friendly Bank is a second mortgage.

If Len stops making payments and the property is sold under power of sale (discussed below), Data Bank of Canada will receive its money first. If there is enough money left over, Friendly Bank will receive its money. For example, assume that Data Bank of Canada's charge is for $220,000, Friendly Bank's charge is for $180,000, and the property sells for $350,000. Data Bank of Canada will receive the first $220,000, and Friendly Bank will receive the balance of $130,000 ($350,000 minus $220,000) because it is second in priority.

Obligations of Mortgagor

Generally, the obligations of the mortgagor include the following:

- *To make all mortgage payments in full and on time.* These payments include all payments of principal and interest to the mortgagee, and to any mortgagees that have priority. For example, if Alan has a first mortgage with Friendly Bank and a second mortgage with Data Bank of Canada, Alan's obligation to Data Bank of Canada is to make payments not only to it, but also to Friendly Bank. In other words, since Friendly Bank has priority, Alan's obligations to Data Bank (second mortgagee) include an obligation to make payments to Friendly Bank (first mortgagee).
- *To maintain fire insurance on the mortgaged property.*

- *To pay all realty taxes.* Since realty taxes have first priority on land, a mortgagor must make sure to pay realty taxes as they become due so that the tax department does not start any default proceedings for unpaid taxes.
- *To keep the mortgaged property in good condition so that its value does not decrease.* For example, if the mortgagor decides that he or she does not want to have a garage attached to his or her property, he or she cannot tear it down without first asking the mortgagee for permission to do so. Tearing down the garage might diminish the value of the property.

Discharge of a Mortgage

When a charge has been paid in full, a document called a **discharge of charge/ mortgage** must be registered on title. Registration of a discharge will extinguish the mortgagee's interest in the property.

Prior to making the final payment, the mortgagor should obtain a discharge statement from the mortgagee confirming the exact amount owing on the charge as of the anticipated payment date.

discharge of charge/ mortgage
a document registered on title when a charge is paid off; given by the chargee to the chargor confirming that the loan has been paid in full and extinguishing the chargee's interest in the property

Default Remedies

Default occurs when the chargor breaches one or more of the obligations contained in the charge. The most obvious and most common form of default is the failure to pay principal and interest payments when due.

Other breaches that can be classified as default include

- failure to have adequate fire insurance on the property,
- failure to pay property taxes, and
- failure to keep the premises in a reasonable state of repair.

In the event of default, the acceleration clause in the charge will permit the chargee to demand immediate payment of the full amount of the loan. In most cases, the chargor will not be able to pay the amount owing and the chargee can then choose from one of the available default remedies. The chargee can sue the chargor for payment of the debt secured by the charge and hope to recover on the judgment.

Typically, however, the chargee will choose a remedy that involves realizing on the secured property—that is, using the property to recover the debt. The chargee will either

- sell the charged property, either through power-of-sale provisions contained in the charge or pursuant to a judicial sale action, or
- obtain title to the charged property by means of a foreclosure action.

There are many business and legal issues to consider when trying to choose the appropriate remedy. Below we discuss the main features of each remedy.

Power of Sale

This remedy permits the chargee to sell the charged property to a third party. The purchaser, in such a case, obtains good title, free and clear of the chargor's interest in the property. This is the remedy used in the majority of cases, since it is relatively quick, inexpensive, and simple to implement.

Except in very rare circumstances, the charge must be in default for at least 15 days before the chargee can commence power-of-sale proceedings. The chargee then serves the chargor with a **notice of sale under mortgage**, indicating the particulars of the default and the amounts owing under the charge. The notice should also be served on

- the spouse of the chargor,
- all subsequent chargees,
- the chargor's execution creditors,
- the lawyer for any construction lien claimants, and
- any other person with an interest in the charged property.

The notice must allow the chargor at least 35 days either to put the charge back into good standing or to pay off the loan completely.

During this 35-day period, the chargee cannot take any steps to sell the property. For example, he/she cannot advertise the property for sale or hire an agent to sell the property. This period is called the **redemption period**. If the charge is still in default after the 35-day period expires, the chargee can then proceed to sell the property.

Until the property is sold, the chargor has the right to put the charge back into good standing and redeem the property. However, as soon as an agreement of purchase and sale is signed, the chargor loses the right to redeem the property.

Once the property is sold, the chargee is required to apply the proceeds to pay off the outstanding debt including all costs incurred in the sale. The chargee is accountable to the chargor and subsequent **encumbrancers** for any **surplus** realized upon the sale of the property. If the proceeds of sale are less than the debt, the chargee can sue the chargor for the deficiency.

The person who buys the property under **power of sale** acquires good title to the property, provided that the sale was properly conducted and that all appropriate parties were duly served with the notice of sale.

Foreclosure

The chargee can commence a court action for a judgment for **foreclosure**, which gives legal title of the property to the chargee. Once the chargee becomes the registered owner of the property, he/she is no longer accountable to the chargor or other subsequent encumbrancers. Their rights will have been extinguished by the final order for foreclosure. This means that if the chargee eventually sells the mortgaged property and the proceeds are more than the amount of the debt, the chargee can keep the surplus. The chargee does not have to pay the surplus to any subsequent encumbrancers or to the chargor.

---

notice of sale under mortgage
a form served when the mortgagee commences power-of-sale proceedings

redemption period
the 35-day period, after the chargor is in default, during which the chargor has the opportunity to put the charge back into good standing and redeem the property, and the chargee cannot take any steps to redeem the property

encumbrancer
a party who has a charge, claim, or lien registered against someone's real property

surplus
an amount left over after paying the mortgage, following a sale under power of sale

power of sale
the power to exercise the remedy of sale in case of default under a charge (for example, the mortgagee can sell the property to a third party when the mortgagor is in default)

foreclosure
a court action whereby the chargee obtains legal title to the property after default by the chargor

Similarly, the chargor is no longer accountable to the chargee in the event that the proceeds from a subsequent sale of the property are less than the amount of the debt. The chargor and any other chargee can defend the foreclosure action or request time to bring the charge back into good standing. They can also request that the property be sold instead. By requesting a sale, the chargor converts the foreclosure action into a normal sale, and any profit will then be applied to pay subsequent encumbrancers, with any remaining money going to the chargor. A chargor will defend the foreclosure action when there is a lot of equity in the property. This will prevent the chargee from gaining a windfall by selling the property and keeping the entire profit.

For example, assume Friendly Bank has a mortgage in the amount of $220,000 on a property that is worth $400,000. If Friendly Bank forecloses on the property and then sells it for $400,000, Friendly Bank can keep the $180,000 profit it makes on the sale. If, however, the chargor defends the foreclosure action and asks the court to convert the foreclosure action into a sale, then Friendly Bank will receive only the amount owing to it, but not more. Friendly Bank can keep $220,000, and the remaining $180,000 will be paid to any subsequent mortgagees, if any. If there is anything left, it goes to the chargor.

By requesting a sale, the chargor releases him/herself from the claims of all other chargees to the extent that the sale money will cover. If the chargor requests time to pay but fails to do so within the time permitted by the court (usually six months) then the chargee can apply for a final order of foreclosure.

Judicial Sale

In a **judicial sale**, the court orders the sale of the property and oversees all matters related to the sale. The sheriff carries out the sale by tender or public auction under the authority of a writ of seizure and sale. A chargee can start an action for a judicial sale, but, more commonly, a judicial sale takes place when a chargor asks that a foreclosure action be converted to a judicial sale.

judicial sale
the sale of charged property ordered and administered by a court

The proceeds from a judicial sale are applied first against the charge debt and any expenses of the sale. Any surplus will then be applied against the amount outstanding on any subsequent charges. The balance, if any, will go to the chargor.

KEY TERMS

amortization period, 73
assuming a mortgage, 71
balance due date, 77
balloon payment, 73
blended payment, 73
closed mortgage, 75
covenant, 72
discharge of charge/
  mortgage, 79
encumbrancer, 80
equity, 70
fixed interest rate, 69
foreclosure, 80

institutional lender, 68
interest, 69
interest adjustment date (IAD), 77
interest rate, 68
judicial sale, 81
mortgage/charge, 68
mortgagee/chargee, 68
mortgagor/chargor, 68
non-blended payment, 75
notice of sale under mortgage, 80
open mortgage, 75
partially open mortgage, 76
power of sale, 80

prepayment penalty, 72
prime lending rate, 69
principal, 69
priority, 78
private lender, 68
redemption period, 80
refinance, 68
security, 68
standard charge terms, 77
surplus, 80
term, 73
variable interest rate, 69
vendor take-back mortgage, 72

REVIEW QUESTIONS

1. Frank borrowed money from Friendly Bank and gave Friendly Bank a charge on his property. Who is the chargor, and who is the chargee? *chargor Frank   Chargee Friendly bank*

2. A mortgage has a 5-year term and a 25-year amortization period. What will happen at the end of the term? Explain your answer.

3. Anita has a closed charge with her bank. She has just won the lottery and wants to pay off the charge. Can she do this? Explain your answer.

4. In addition to making regular mortgage payments, what obligations does the mortgagor have?

5. Lorne has a mortgage with ABC Bank, with an interest rate of prime plus 2 percent. Is this a fixed rate or a variable rate? Explain your answer.

6. Lynne sold her house to Bill and lent him $200,000 so that he could complete the sale. How should Lynne secure this loan?

7. David arranges a mortgage on June 15. His mortgage payments are due on the first day of each month.

   a. What is the interest adjustment date?

   b. What is the first regular mortgage payment date?

8. What is the name of the document that is registered when a mortgage is paid in full?

9. Sanjaya wants to buy Sheila's home. There is an outstanding mortgage on the property that has a very low interest rate. What is the best option for Sanjaya and Sheila in this situation with respect to the outstanding mortgage?

10. Aahmad has not made a mortgage payment to ABC Bank in two months. What is the least expensive and most efficient mortgage remedy for ABC Bank to use in this situation? *Power of Sale*

Intellectual Property

6

LEARNING OUTCOMES

After reading this chapter, you should be able to:

- Understand the concept of intellectual property
- Explain how intellectual property rights arise
- Identify the various types of intellectual property and understand the differences between them
- Understand the legal protections available for the different types of intellectual property
- Explain how to enforce intellectual property rights
- Describe the various symbols used to identify intellectual property protection

Introduction

In Chapter 4, we discussed real property and the rights associated with ownership of this type of property. As we saw, determining ownership is fairly straightforward; whoever has the fee simple estate in the real property is the legal owner.

In this chapter we focus on a different type of property—**intellectual property** (or IP). Unlike real property (and personal property), this type of property cannot be described by its boundaries and dimensions or other physical attributes—for example, its size or its colour. Intellectual property is "a creation or invention of the mind." Unlike other kinds of property, IP has no palpable, material existence, but it does exist. In fact, we are surrounded by evidence of it in our everyday lives. The music we listen to; the books we read; the movies we watch; the design, image, or logo that differentiates our favourite brand of take-out coffee; the computer software we rely on—these are all examples of intellectual property. They are all the result or outcome of some mind's creation or invention. For this reason, ownership of intellectual property is really ownership of an intangible "idea" or "concept." And, as with real property, the law recognizes and protects ownership rights associated with intellectual property. The law gives the owner an exclusive right to use his/her intellectual property, including the right to deal with it, to sell it, or to allow someone else to use it. In this respect, IP is just like any other type of property.

An owner of intellectual property typically wants legal protection against his/her idea or creation being used or copied without permission. An idea itself is not protected. In other words, if you are simply thinking about creating a product, your thoughts alone cannot be protected. However, as soon as you act on them—by designing an image, inventing a product, or writing a song, for example—they become intellectual property and are entitled to protection. In this chapter, we look at four types of intellectual property:

1. copyright,
2. patents,
3. trademarks, and
4. industrial designs.

These are all valuable forms of intellectual property. In the same way that a landowner protects his/her "title" to real property, so too should a creator protect his/her intellectual property rights. As you read, keep in mind that the different types of intellectual property often overlap. In other words, some creations or inventions call for more than one type of intellectual property protection.

Types of Intellectual Property

Copyright

Copyright is the way writers, artists, and musicians protect their original work, which is a form of intellectual property. Copyright literally means just that (that is, the right to copy), and the owner of the copyright is the only one who has the right to copy his or her work.

Copyright extends to any form of literary, artistic, dramatic, or musical work—for example, novels, textbooks, manuscripts, computer programs, paintings, sculptures, photographs, illustrations, plays, films, scripts, songs, and musical compositions. The law governing copyright in Canada is the federal *Copyright Act*.[1] Under this statute, copyright extends to the expression of an idea, not to the idea itself. In other words, if someone writes a book about how to train a puppy, he or she cannot protect that idea; anyone else can write a book about how to train a puppy, without violating any copyright. However, copyright will protect the way in which the idea is conveyed; it will prevent anyone from copying the exact expression of someone else's idea.

For example, if a person copied the book on how to train a puppy, but changed only the cover and called it "How to Train a Puppy, 2nd edition," that person would be violating copyright.

Under the *Copyright Act*, a work must meet certain criteria in order to qualify for copyright recognition and protection. The work must be

- original—it cannot be a copy of someone else's work, and
- expressed in a fixed form—a thought or idea will not attract copyright; it must be written down or recorded.

Under the *Copyright Act*, the owner of the copyright in an eligible work has

> the sole right to produce or reproduce the work or any substantial part thereof in any material form whatever, to perform the work or any substantial part thereof in public or, if the work is unpublished, to publish the work or any substantial part thereof.[2]

The owner of the copyright is usually the author of an original work. However, if the author assigns ownership of the work, the person to whom the author assigns the copyright will be the owner. Also, if the author creates the work in the course of his/her employment, then the author's employer will own the copyright, unless there is an agreement to the contrary.

For example, assume Jayme is a musician and composes a song in his spare time. He is the author of the work as well as the copyright owner. If Jayme assigns his ownership to Belinda, then Jayme is the author of the work, but Belinda is the copyright owner. If Jayme composed the song during working hours, as part of his

copyright
the exclusive "right to copy" a writer's, artist's, or musician's original work

---

1   RSC 1985, c. C-42.

2   Ibid., s. 3(1).

employment duties, then he is the author, but his employer is the copyright owner (assuming there is no agreement that states otherwise). It is important to determine who the copyright owner is because only that person has the exclusive right to produce or reproduce all (or a substantial part of) the work, in any form.

Copyright is infringed if someone (other than the owner) does anything that only the owner of the copyright can do, without the owner's consent. For example, assume that Myjan owns the copyright in a children's book he wrote. If anyone else copied all of Myjan's book, or even a very distinctive part of it, then that person is violating Myjan's ownership rights of his book. Such a violation is referred to as an **infringement of copyright**.

In some situations, use of someone else's copyright will not be considered an infringement of copyright. The *Copyright Act* sets out specific circumstances in which anyone can use copyrighted material, without permission. These are known as **fair dealing exemptions**, and they permit use of someone else's copyrighted work for research, private study, education, criticism or review, and news reporting. If the user can demonstrate that his or her use falls within one of the fair dealing exemptions specified in the statute, then the use will not be an infringement of copyright.

For example, the statute permits people to reproduce or copy a computer program, for backup purposes.[3] Fair dealing exemptions cover situations where the purpose of the dealing is not for commercial gain, but rather for private purposes that will not affect the copyright owner in a negative way, financially or otherwise. In these situations, there will not be an infringement of copyright.

Copyright protection arises automatically; the author of the work does not have to do anything. And it lasts for the duration of the author's life, plus an additional 50 years. This means that the family members of the author of the copyright are protected as well, long after the death of the author.

A copyright owner in Canada may register his/her copyright with the Canadian Intellectual Property Office (CIPO). Although registration is not mandatory, a certificate of registration provides evidence of copyright protection and ownership. This may become important in a case where the copyright owner is someone other than the author of the original work.

A copyright symbol may be used within a work to indicate that the work is protected by copyright. This is not required to enforce copyright in Canada, but it may help with international protection of a work. It also prevents anyone from claiming that he/she was unaware of a copyright. The copyright owner should clearly mark the work with the symbol ©, followed by his/her name and the year in which the work was created.

The remedy for infringement of a copyright is typically an award of damages to the copyright owner, to compensate him or her for the losses suffered as a result of the infringement. The amount awarded will take into consideration profits earned by the infringer. Rather than requiring the copyright owner to accept damages based on the loss of profit, the *Copyright Act* permits a copyright owner to choose instead an

infringement of copyright
occurs when someone (other than the copyright owner) does something that only the copyright owner can do, without the owner's permission

fair dealing exemptions
uses of someone else's copyright that are not considered an infringement of copyright

---

3 Ibid., s. 30.6.

award of statutory damages of up to $20,000 (if the infringement was for commercial purposes) or $5,000 (if the infringement was for non-commercial purposes).

Finally, it should be noted that unauthorized recording of a movie in a movie theatre for the purpose of selling, renting, or commercially distributing it is a crime in Canada, punishable by imprisonment for up to five years.[4]

Patents

A **patent** is the way inventors protect their inventions, which represent another form of intellectual property. A patent (also known as **letters patent**) is granted by the government. This patent gives the creator of an invention the exclusive right to produce, use, sell, or otherwise take advantage of his or her new invention for a period of 20 years. No one else can use the invention during this period without obtaining permission from the patent holder. When, after 20 years, the patent expires, everyone is then free to create copies of the invention in his/her own format.

The law governing patents in Canada is the federal *Patent Act*.[5] This statute defines an invention as "any new and useful art, process, machine, manufacture or composition of matter, or any new and useful improvement in any art, process, machine, manufacture or composition of matter."[6] As you can see, the definition of invention is very broad and covers many different types of inventions—for example, a method or process of removing rust, a machine that cuts metal, and a drug that suppresses appetite (or an improvement on any of these). While there are countless inventions created, not all of them are eligible for patent protection. To be granted a patent, the invention must be

- new—that is, the first of its kind in the world, and not already disclosed to the public (anywhere in the world) by a third party;
- useful and functional—have a useful purpose, and work properly (that is, it performs its intended purpose); and
- inventive or ingenious—not obvious to someone skilled in the same field.

For example, a pen that never runs out of ink because it continually generates new ink, and a light bulb that never burns out, are examples of products that might be patentable inventions.

The rationale for protecting creators of new ideas is that such protection encourages the invention of new products that will benefit the public. Many people would love to have a pen that never runs out, or a light bulb that never has to be changed. The Post-it Note is an example of an invention that met the eligibility criteria above. Until the patent expired, the inventor had a monopoly on all the profits—he was the only one who could sell this innovative and useful invention. Today, others copy this invention and offer it for sale. However, many people continue to choose the original

patent
an exclusive right (granted by the government upon application by an inventor) to produce, use, sell, or otherwise take advantage of an invention for a period of 20 years

letters patent
another term for patent

---

4   *Criminal Code*, RSC 1985, c. C-46, s. 432.

5   RSC 1985, c. P-4.

6   Ibid., s. 2.

brand. The patent gives an inventor a huge marketing advantage and is the main reason to seek patent protection for eligible inventions.

Patent protection, unlike copyright, does not arise automatically. An inventor must file an application with the Canadian Intellectual Property Office (CIPO). Applications are granted on a first-to-file system. This means that if two people independently invent the same machine, priority is given to the first person to file an application for a patent, not the first person to invent the machine. Before applying for a patent, it is a good idea to conduct a preliminary search of existing patents to determine whether your invention is actually "new." You can't patent an invention that already has a patent.

When applying for a patent, the inventor must submit a completed application form and pay the required fee. The application must contain a detailed description of the invention, known as the **specification**, as well as a **petition**—a formal request to the Commissioner of Patents to grant a patent. The specification must include the **inventor's claims**. This is the part of the specification that defines the boundaries of an inventor's patent protection. The claims let others know the extent of patent protection and what aspects of the invention cannot legally be used before the patent expires. For example, when the Post-it Note was patented, it presumably described the invention as a pad of sticky pieces of paper in various shapes and colours. If someone else created a colourful pad of paper, without the sticky component, the patent would make it clear that the pad of paper was not in violation of the Post-it patent.

Patent applications are costly and quite complicated. Many inventors hire a **registered patent agent** to represent them in these applications. Registered patent agents specialize in patent applications and have training in patent law and procedure.

Once a patent is granted, only the patent holder has the right to produce, use, and sell the invention. The patent holder can either produce the product him/herself or permit someone else to produce it on his or her behalf. For example, if Marlene creates the light bulb that never burns out, she can sell Judith the rights to actually produce it. If anyone else interferes with the patent holder's exclusive rights to the invention—by, for example, producing or selling the patented invention without permission—**patent infringement** has occurred. The *Patent Act* provides that "a person who infringes a patent is liable to the patentee and to all persons claiming under the patentee for all damage sustained by the patentee or by any such person, after the grant of the patent, by reason of the infringement."[7] The infringer is typically required to pay the patent holder (patentee) any profits earned, as well as damages. In addition, the patentee can seek an **injunction** to prevent further infringement.

While a patent application is pending, the inventor may put the words "patent pending" on any merchandise that is produced. This has no legal effect, but it tells everyone that there will likely soon be patent protection for this merchandise. Once the patent is granted, the inventor may (but is not required to) put the word "patented" on the invention, together with the patent number.

specification
a detailed description of the invention contained in an application for a patent

petition
a formal request to the Commissioner of Patents to grant a patent

inventor's claims
the claims included in the specification; defines the boundaries of an inventor's patent protection

registered patent agent
a person who has training in patent law and specializes in patent applications

patent infringement
interference with the patent holder's exclusive rights to produce, use, sell, or otherwise take advantage of his/her patented invention, without permission

injunction
a court order requiring a party to refrain from doing a specific act

---

7   Ibid., s. 55(1).

As mentioned above, the term of a patent is 20 years from the date the application is filed. Patent protection applies only within the country that grants a patent. If, for example, an inventor obtains a Canadian patent for his or her invention, the patent will not prevent someone in the United States from reproducing the invention, unless the inventor has also obtained a United States patent. A patent cannot be renewed. It gives the creator only 20 years in which to have a monopoly over the invention and to win over the market for that product. After 20 years, the creator's exclusive right is extinguished, and the public is free to create identical products that compete with the original. The right to compete is beneficial to the public because it permits other inventors to create products that are similar to the original and may be more functional and/or less expensive. For example, there are many types of sticky pads of paper available today, some of which are arguably more functional than the original Post-it Note and some that are also less expensive.

Trademarks

A **trademark** is a word (or words), design, slogan, symbol, logo, or any other mark (or a combination of these) that identifies and distinguishes one person's goods or services from those of all others. A trademark could also apply to a unique way of packaging goods—for example, the Coca-Cola bottle. People associate a particular trademark with the reputation of a company and the reliability and quality of its brand or product. For example, most people associate the Mercedes and Lexus trademarks with prestige and luxury. If you are purchasing a new smartphone, the BlackBerry and Apple trademarks will easily identify those brands. And most of us are familiar with the distinctive marks used by Roots and Lululemon that distinguish their brand from all others. As you can see, trademarks are a very valuable type of intellectual property and therefore should be protected.

Trade names are very similar in nature to trademarks. A **trade name** (also known as a business name) is the name that a sole proprietorship, partnership, or corporation uses to carry on business. As we saw in Chapter 1, if a sole proprietor runs a business using the name "Bryce's Helping Hands," that name is known as both a business name and a trade name. As is the case with trademarks, trade names can identify and distinguish a particular business from all others, and are therefore also protected under trademark law. For example, most people associate the names Esso and Shell with popular gas stations in Ontario. The law governing the registration, use, and protection of trademarks in Canada is the federal *Trade-marks Act*.[8]

To register a trademark with the Canadian Intellectual Property Office, the applicant must establish that the trademark is

- already being used in Canada (or will be in use by the time of registration);
- distinctive, and not merely descriptive of the goods or services; and
- registrable—in other words, it meets the registration requirements set out in the *Trade-marks Act*.

trademark
a word(s), design, slogan, symbol, logo, or any other mark (or a combination of these) that identifies and distinguishes a person's goods or services from those of all others

trade name
the name that a sole proprietorship, partnership, or corporation uses to carry on business

---

8 RSC 1985, c. T-13.

A distinctive trademark is one that permits everyone to easily distinguish and identify the source of the goods or services associated with that trademark. For example, people associate the trademark "BlackBerry" with the smartphone or tablet produced by Research in Motion (RIM). Words that describe goods or services as "fast" or "easy" are generally not registrable. The trademark "fast smartphone," for example, is descriptive, but not distinctive—it does not identify a specific brand or source. It is therefore not a registrable trademark. However, if someone used this name over a period of time and people started associating "fast smartphone" with one particular brand or product, then the trademark might be considered distinctive and, therefore, registrable.

The *Trade-marks Act* sets out other requirements for registrability.[9] Generally, a trademark is not registrable if it is

- mostly made up of the name or surname of someone who is alive, or who died within the preceding 30 years (for example, "Rajad," or "Rajad Singh");
- merely descriptive (as discussed above);
- clearly misleading—in other words, deceptively misdescribing the character or quality of the goods or services or their place of origin (for example, applying the phrase "Italian Luggage" to goods manufactured in China);
- the name (in any language) of any goods or services associated with the use of the trademark (for example, "telefono inteligente," Spanish for smartphone, could not be a registrable trademark for a smartphone);
- too similar to and/or easily confused with an existing registered trademark or a pending one (for example, "BerryBlack" for a smartphone; or "Tom Horton's" for coffee);
- a name well known as the place of origin of the goods or services being trademarked (for example, using the name "China" for a service that produces Chinese food);
- similar to an official design (for example, the Canadian flag, or Ontario's white trillium); or
- considered immoral, obscene, or scandalous (for example, containing offensive language or images).

The *Trade-marks Act* makes an exception in certain circumstances for a trademark that is descriptive only or that is merely someone's name or surname. Pursuant to s. 12(2), a trademark that is otherwise not registrable for either of these reasons "is registrable if it has been so used in Canada by the applicant or his predecessor in title as to have become distinctive at the date of filing an application for its registration." For example, assume Wendi Wolf operates a fur coat business called "Wolf." Because "Wolf" is her surname, it is not a registrable trademark, unless Wendi can establish that "Wolf" has become so well known that everyone associates "Wolf" with her fur coat business.

---

9 Ibid., s. 12.

The owner of a registered trademark has the exclusive right to use the trademark in Canada for a period of 15 years, and it can be renewed every 15 years subsequently. Unlike a patent (which cannot be renewed), a trademark can be renewed indefinitely. This is necessary because a trademark represents a unique way of identifying a product. Allowing others to use the trademark at any time without permission might cause the public to be deceived about the true identity of a competing product.

While there is no legal requirement to register a trademark, use of an unregistered trademark provides common-law protection only. In other words, if there is a dispute about whether someone has the right to use a trademark, the owner of an unregistered trademark must prove ownership. This may result in lengthy and expensive legal proceedings. Once a trademark is registered, however, it constitutes proof of ownership. As stated in the *Trade-marks Act*, the "right of the owner of a registered trademark to its exclusive use shall be deemed to be infringed by a person not entitled to its use under this Act who sells, distributes or advertises wares or services in association with a confusing trade-mark or trade-name."[10]

As you can see, registration provides the exclusive right to use the trademark throughout Canada. If another person uses a mark or name that is so similar to the registered trademark that it will likely cause confusion about the source of the goods or services, this is considered an infringement of trademark.

It is also considered to be infringement if someone uses another person's registered trademark in such a way that it potentially diminishes the public goodwill toward either the trademark owner or the reputation of his/her goods or services.

Trademarks that are not registered are also protected at law. Use of someone's unregistered trademark may establish a cause of action against the unauthorized user for the common-law tort of "passing off." This tort, as one legal scholar has defined it,

> consists of the making of some false representation to the public, or to third persons, likely to induce them to believe that the goods or services of another are those of the plaintiff. This may be done, for example, by counterfeiting or imitating the plaintiff's trade mark or trade name, his wrappers, labels or containers, his vehicles, the badges or uniforms of his employees, or the appearance of his place of business. The test laid down in such cases has been whether the resemblance is so great as to deceive the ordinary customer acting with the caution usually exercised in such transactions, so that he may mistake one for the other.[11]

This is very similar to an action for infringement under s. 7 of the *Trade-marks Act*, but can also involve claims related to the likely confusion or misleading of the consumer rather than to actual use of a registered trademark. Passing-off claims may concern, for example, misleading advertising, copying the distinctive design or packaging of someone else's product, or using unregistered marks. To succeed in a common-law passing-off action, the plaintiff must establish "(a) the existence of goodwill [the intangible component of the value of a business, such as its reputation];

---

10   Ibid., s. 20(1).

11   William L. Prosser, *The Law of Torts* (4th ed.), cited in *Consumers Distributing Co. v. Seiko Time Canada Ltd.*, [1984] 1 SCR 583.

(b) deception of the public due to a misrepresentation; and (c) actual or potential damage to the plaintiff."[12] These elements are often very difficult to prove at trial and can result in lengthy and expensive litigation.

Enforcement by owners of a registered trademark is far simpler. This is because once a trademark is registered, the goodwill associated with that trademark is assumed. Furthermore, in an action for infringement, damage is presumed to have occurred as soon as the element of deception or confusion is established. Therefore, it is always advisable to register a trademark if possible.

A statutory action for trademark infringement often accompanies an action for the common-law tort of passing off. For example, assume someone opens a gas station called Shell-O Gas and uses a yellow shell design that is very similar to the Shell logo we are all familiar with. In this situation, in addition to bringing an action for infringement of trademark, the owner of the Shell trademark should include a claim for passing off. The owner should do so for the following reason. The court may determine that the names and the logos are different enough and that there is no likelihood of confusing the two gas stations. In this case, the action for infringement would be unsuccessful. In this event, the owner of the Shell trademark can then pursue the passing-off action.

In some cases, a common-law action for passing off is the only option available. For instance, if a trademark is not registered, there can be no "infringement" and therefore no action under the *Trade-marks Act*. Many businesses operate using names that are not registrable, and therefore not protected by trademark. For example, as mentioned above, a trademark is not registrable if it is made up of the surname of someone who is alive. If Devon Baker uses the name "Baker Bread" for his frozen bread business, he cannot register the business/trade name as a trademark (assuming it does not fall within the exception discussed above). Therefore, if someone starts a frozen bread business using a very similar name, Devon's only recourse is to bring an action for passing off. Because the trademark is not registered, he cannot bring an action for infringement.

The remedies for trademark infringement typically include

- the injunction—a court order requiring the infringer to stop using the trademark; and
- damages—compensating the owner of the registered trademark for loss suffered, including loss of goodwill or reputation (which should include an amount for profits earned by the infringer).

The remedies sought in a passing-off claim are virtually the same as those for trademark infringement.

Although not mandatory, a trademark symbol may accompany a trademark, whether or not the trademark is registered. For an unregistered trademark, the symbol used is ™; it lets people know you are claiming common-law rights to the trademark. For a trademark that is registered, the symbol ® can be used. This symbol lets people know you are the legal owner of the registered trademark.

---

12 *Ciba-Geigy Canada Ltd. v. Apotex Inc.*, [1992] 3 SCR 120.

Industrial Design

Industrial design refers to the way a finished product *looks*—that is, its "visual appeal," not the way it functions. Industrial design means the "features of shape, configuration, pattern or ornament and any combination of those features that, in a finished article, appeal to and are judged solely by the eye."[13] A product's design may include very important functional aspects, but industrial design refers only to the aesthetic aspects of a finished product. The visual lines of an iMac computer, the shape of a specific brand of perfume bottle, and the particular shape of a barstool—these are examples of industrial design. Since the design of the iMac computer is purely aesthetic and unrelated to its function, it qualifies as an industrial design. As you can imagine, a product that has a visually appealing design is likely to attract more interest. Perfume bottles are typically very unique in shape and colour and can in themselves identify a particular brand. An industrial design can therefore be a valuable type of intellectual property and, like the other forms of intellectual property, should be protected.

> **industrial design**
> the aesthetic aspects of a finished product; its visual appeal, not its function

Industrial designs are governed by the federal *Industrial Design Act*.[14] Under this statute, registration provides the owner of an industrial design with the exclusive right to use the design for a period of 10 years. During this time, no one is allowed to copy the design. After this time, however, anyone may make, import, rent, or sell the design in Canada.

An industrial design can be registered at any time as long as the design is original and has not been made public (that is, published). Once an industrial design is published, it must be registered by a date no later than 12 months after the date of publication.

As already mentioned, registration protects an industrial design by preventing anyone besides the owner from using or copying the design, without permission. The owner has the exclusive right to use the registered industrial design and can bring an action for infringement against any unauthorized user of it. The remedy for infringement is set out in the *Industrial Design Act*, which provides that "in any proceedings under section 15, the court may make such orders as the circumstances require, including orders for relief by way of injunction and the recovery of damages or profits, for punitive damages, and for the disposal of any infringing article or kit."[15]

Although not required, a symbol may be used to alert others that a product's industrial design has been registered and is therefore protected. The symbol for a registered industrial design is an uppercase "D" inserted in a circle, followed by the owner's name.

---

13   *Industrial Design Act*, RSC 1985, c. I-9.

14   Ibid.

15   Ibid., s. 15.1.

Summary Scenario: The Various Types of Intellectual Property

Let's look at a scenario that illustrates the different types of intellectual property discussed in this chapter.

Judene has created an innovative product that she is certain many people will want to buy. It is a mug that continually heats any hot drink it contains. Judene is certain that coffee lovers, especially, will want to buy this product so that they never have to worry about their coffee getting cold. When not in use, the mug is meant to be stored in a very unique, colourful, and visually distinctive base that, when turned upside down, becomes an airtight cover to the mug. This allows people to carry the mug around without worrying about the contents spilling out. Judene has also designed and written a small information booklet (included with each mug) that illustrates how to convert the base into a decorative cover and how to properly insert the mug into the base when not in use. She wants to call her new invention the "Hottee Koffee Mugg."

Judene's invention is an example of intellectual property. It is a creation of the mind, and it may qualify for all four types of intellectual property protection. Consider the following:

1. The mug is likely a patentable invention; it is new, useful, and arguably inventive.
2. The unique shape of the coffee mug's base, together with its colourful and fancy-looking design, may qualify it as an industrial design.
3. Her proposed name for the mug (that is, Hottee Koffee Mugg) meets the criteria for a registrable trademark and may therefore qualify as a trademark that Judene can register.
4. Judene's information booklet will qualify for copyright protection, together with any other written information she may develop to promote her Hottee Koffee Mugg.

As you can see from this example, it is possible for a single product to require more than one type of IP protection.

Figure 6.1　Types of Intellectual Property

	Copyright	Patent	Trademark	Industrial Design
Deals with	Literary, artistic, dramatic, and musical works (expression of an idea)	Inventions	Word(s), design, symbol, slogan, logo, or any other mark (or combination of these) that distinguishes goods or services	• Shape, configuration, pattern, or ornament • Appearance of object, not its function
Requirements	Original and expressed in a fixed form	New, useful, and inventive	• Already in use • Distinctive • Registrable	• Original • Not public knowledge
Protection	• Arises automatically • Exclusive right to copy and use the idea • Registration is optional	• Must apply for protection • Exclusive right to produce, sell, and use invention	• Must apply for protection • Exclusive right to use trademark	• Must apply for protection • Exclusive right to use, sell, and manufacture design
Term of Protection	Author's life plus 50 years	20 years	15 years, and can be renewed every 15 years	10 years
Symbol Used	© (if registered)	Patent Pending Patented	™ (unregistered) ® (registered)	"D" inserted in a circle
Statute	*Copyright Act*	*Patent Act*	*Trade-marks Act*	*Industrial Design Act*
Reminder: There is no protection or monopoly in an idea				

KEY TERMS

copyright, 85
fair dealing exemptions, 86
industrial design, 93
infringement of copyright, 86
injunction, 88

intellectual property, 84
inventor's claims, 88
letters patent, 87
patent, 87
patent infringement, 88

petition, 88
registered patent agent, 88
specification, 88
trade name, 89
trademark, 89

REVIEW QUESTIONS

1. State the four different types of intellectual property. •
   Copyright, Patents, trademark, industrial

2. What type of protection is available to a symbol that
   identifies a particular brand of running shoe?
   trademark

3. Someone has created a smartphone that has a built-
   in adjustable wrist strap with an extremely
   interesting design and colour. What type of
   intellectual property is this an example of?

4. For each of the following product names, state
   whether or not it is a registrable trademark. Explain
   your answer.

   • "Spicy Sauce," for a spicy-tasting sauce *NO*

   • "App-le," for an electronic device *no*

   • "Barbecue Brothers," for a barbecue cleaning
     and repair service *Yes*

5. Sam is researching cancer treatments. He found some
   material written by Alonzo and wants to share that
   information with his family. Is this an infringement of
   Alonzo's intellectual property rights? Explain your
   answer.
   *No as he is only sharing
   Alonzo research as he
   is not cliam it for his own
   or adding anything he's
   just sharing the treatment
   research.*

design → fair dealing exemptions

6. Jumil invented the light bulb that never burns out
   and obtained patent protection for it this year. When,
   if ever, can someone copy this idea and create a
   similar product? *after 20 yrs*

7. What remedies are available for infringement of a
   copyright? *damages to compensate*

8. Harvey published a novel last year, shortly before he
   died. He never applied for copyright protection. His
   family wants to know whether or not Harvey's novel
   has copyright protection and, if so, how long
   copyright protection will last. *50yrs they can
   do a search at CIPO*

9. Phyllis registered an industrial design yesterday. How
   long will her intellectual property rights in the
   industrial design be protected?
   10 yrs $after

*however they don't need to do
anything as it's done automatically*

*3.
→ intellectual property it is creation of the mind and it
may qualify for all 4 types of intellectual property
- design design   - patents
- copyright   - industrial design*

PART III

Estate Planning and Administration

In Part III of this text, we discuss what happens to a person's property if he or she dies or becomes incapable of managing his or her affairs. We begin with a discussion of wills—that is, the legal documents that people use to plan ahead and control how all of their property is distributed when they die. Chapter 7 explains basic will terminology and describes the formal requirements of a valid will. We examine the most common clauses contained in a will and discuss a holograph will—a type of will that is entirely in a person's own handwriting. We also explain what happens to a person's property—in other words, his or her estate—when that person dies without a will. We look at how to challenge the validity of a will. The chapter ends with a discussion of the various claims that can be made against an estate.

In Chapter 8, we deal with the administration of a person's estate upon death. We look at the legal require-ment to appoint an estate trustee—in other words, the person or persons who actually administer the estate of someone who died, whether or not the deceased has left a will. We also discuss probate, which is an import-ant and often costly element of estate administration, and we consider ways to avoid probate. Lastly, we ex-amine what happens when gifts in a will are no longer available.

In Chapter 9, we deal with the power of attorney—that is, the legal document people use to plan ahead not for death, but for a time when they may no longer be capable of making their own decisions about their property or their personal care. We explain how people can appoint someone they trust to act on their behalf and make binding decisions for them, in the event they are incapable or otherwise unavailable to act for themselves.

Wills

7

LEARNING OUTCOMES

After reading this chapter, you should be able to:

- Understand will terminology
- Describe the difference between specific bequests and the residue of an estate
- Explain the formal requirements of a valid will
- Understand codicils and how they differ from a will
- Understand the most common will provisions
- Understand the meaning of intestacy, and how an estate is distributed when a person dies without a will
- Describe the different kinds of claims that can be made against an estate

Introduction

will/last will and testament
a written document that dictates what happens to a person's estate when the person dies

estate
the total of everything a person owned immediately before he or she died

executed
signed by the testator and witnessed by two people who are present at the same time as the testator

testator
a person who dies with a valid will

estate trustee
a person who is appointed to carry out the instructions of a deceased person

beneficiary
an entity that receives a gift under a will

A **will**, also known as a **last will and testament**, is a document that dictates what happens to a person's **estate** when the person dies. An estate is the total of everything a person owned immediately before he or she died, including real property (for example, a house) and personal property (for example, a car and a bank account). As long as a will is **executed** (that is, properly signed and witnessed) it governs what will happen to each item of property—whether that item will be given to someone, or whether it will be sold and the money paid out to those entitled to receive it. A will also states who will take care of distributing the estate, known as administering the estate. In Ontario, it is not mandatory to have a will, and many people do not. Having a will, however, makes the process of dealing with a deceased person's estate much easier.

A person who dies with a valid will is called a **testator**. In his or her will, the testator appoints a person (or persons) to deal with the estate upon death. That person (or persons) is known as the **estate trustee**. The testator also leaves various gifts (for example, a house, a car, or money) in his or her will, and anyone who is named in the testator's will as the recipient of a gift is referred to as a **beneficiary**. A beneficiary can be a child, sibling, parent, or other relative of the testator. Alternatively, it can be someone unrelated to the testator, such as a caregiver, friend, or anyone else the testator wants to leave a gift to. Charities are often beneficiaries.

Formal Requirements

In order for a will to be valid, it must be properly signed by the testator, and it must be witnessed. These formal requirements exist to ensure that fraud is not committed.

Signing

undue influence
when someone in a position of power exerts pressure on another person to sign a document, even though it may not be in that person's best interest

The testator must sign the will at its end, using his or her normal signature, in the presence of two witnesses. If the testator is incapable of signing, the testator can have someone else who is present sign on his/her behalf. This exception is provided for in the governing statute, the *Succession Law Reform Act*.[1] In this situation, the testator must acknowledge in the presence of the two witnesses that he or she is authorizing the person to sign on his or her behalf. Neither the person who signs on the testator's behalf, nor that person's spouse, can receive any benefit under the will. If they are named as beneficiaries under the will, the will itself remains valid, but the gift to them is deemed to be invalid, unless they can prove that there was no **undue influence**. A testator who is incapable of writing can also sign the will by simply writing an "X" where it says "Name of Testator." In this case, both witnesses must sign an affidavit confirming that the "X" represents the testator's signature.

---

1 RSO 1990, c. S.26, s. 12(3).

Witnesses

In order for a will to be valid, there must be two witnesses, both at least 18 years of age and both present (in the same room and at the same time) when the testator signs the will. One of the witnesses must sign an **affidavit of execution**, swearing to the fact that both witnesses were present at the same time and that they witnessed the testator's signing the will. For example, if Andrew is signing his will in the presence of Breane and Cody, Breane can sign the affidavit swearing to the fact that she and Cody were both present and that together they witnessed Andrew sign the will. Neither a witness, nor the spouse of a witness, can receive any benefit under the will. In other words, a witness cannot be a beneficiary under the will whose signing he or she is witnessing. If a witness is named as a beneficiary in the will, then (as with a gift to a person signing on behalf of the testator) the will itself remains valid, but the gift to the witness will be deemed to be invalid, unless the witness can prove that there was no undue influence.

affidavit of execution
a document that is signed by one of the witnesses to a will and that swears to the fact that both witnesses were present when the will was signed

Testamentary Intent

To be legally valid, the testator must have **testamentary intent**. In other words, the testator must intend for the document to be his or her final will—that is, the final disposition of all his/her property upon death. For example, if Jake gives written instructions to someone about the provisions he wants included in his will, the written instructions do not constitute a valid will because they lack testamentary intent; Jake's intent, in this case, is to provide instructions about his will only.

testamentary intent
the intent to dispose of assets in a will

Holograph Will

A **holograph will** is a will that is entirely in the testator's own handwriting and does not have to meet the formal requirement of having two witnesses. This type of will can be used any time, but is typically used in an emergency situation where there is no time to have a lawyer draft a formal will, or where two witnesses are not available. In this situation, the testator simply writes down his or her final wishes on a piece of paper. The following are the legal requirements for a valid holograph will:

holograph will
a will that is entirely handwritten and signed by the testator (and not witnessed)

- the entire document is handwritten by the deceased;
- the document is signed at the end, and dated; and
- the document contains "a deliberate or fixed and final expression of intention as to the disposal of property upon death."[2] In other words, the testator is stating how to distribute his/her property, as opposed to describing, for example, how to merely maintain or store the property.

---

2 *Bennett v. Toronto General Trusts Corp.; Bennett v. Gray*, [1958] SCR 392, 14 DLR (2d) 1, at 396.

Common Will Provisions

Wills are usually drafted by lawyers, and lawyers must take into account the particular circumstances and wishes of the testator. In other words, each will a lawyer prepares is customized to suit the specific needs of a client. Therefore, each will is unique; no two people will have exactly the same one. However, there are some clauses that are mandatory and others that, although not mandatory, are very common. Let's look at these clauses.

Naming of Estate Trustee(s)

As already mentioned, the testator must name an estate trustee—the person who will administer the estate.

In his or her will, a testator can name either one person alone or multiple persons to act as the estate trustee(s). If there are multiple estate trustees, the will may direct them to act jointly. This means that all of them must be involved in every step of the distribution of the estate, and all of their signatures must appear on every estate-related document. Alternatively, the will may direct that each one of them, on his/her own, has the power to administer the estate without any other estate trustee's signature. When preparing his or her will, the testator has to decide how many estate trustees there should be and, if there are to be more than one, whether or not they must act jointly.

The estate trustee is usually a close relative of the testator—for example, his or her spouse, or child(ren), or the testator's lawyer. For example, assume Arif has two children, a son and a daughter, and he wants both of them to be estate trustees of his will. If he prefers that they always make decisions and sign documents together, then he should appoint both of them and make it clear that they must act jointly. If, on the other hand, his son lives far away and it makes more sense for Arif to give control of the estate's administration to his daughter alone, Arif can name both of them as estate trustees but state that they do not have to act jointly; either his daughter or his son can act independently. It is likely, in this example, that the daughter will do more of the administration because she lives physically closer to Arif than the son does. Nonetheless, Arif shows, by naming both the son and the daughter as estate trustees, that he is treating his children equally.

Where there is only one estate trustee, the testator commonly names someone to act as an alternate estate trustee in the event that the first is unable or unwilling to fulfill the role. For example, assume Arif names his wife Joanie as the estate trustee of his will, and names his son, Shahin, as an alternate estate trustee. If Joanie predeceases (dies before) Arif, Shahin will be the estate trustee of Arif's will. As you can see, it is important to name an alternate estate trustee because it is impossible for a testator to know, when preparing his or her will, whether the estate trustee named will be alive when the testator dies.

Beneficiaries

The beneficiaries are the people who receive a gift (also known as a bequest) under a will. For example, if in his will Jorge leaves his house to his wife, his car to his brother, and $10,000 to his best friend, then his wife, brother, and best friend are all beneficiaries under his will. Gifts of a specific item, such as the house, car, and $10,000, are called **specific bequests**.

When preparing a will, the testator cannot know exactly what property he or she will own upon death. Therefore, a properly drafted will should include a provision that deals with payment of the **residue** of the testator's estate. The residue is everything that is left over after all of the debts and expenses have been paid and the specific gifts, of either actual items or money, have been distributed. Let's return to the above example. If Jorge had $50,000 in the bank, a second car, and some jewellery, the sum of $40,000 ($50,000 minus the $10,000 given to his best friend), the second car, and the jewellery would form the residue of his estate. Depending on how a will is worded, the residue of the estate may be sold or **liquidated**, and the proceeds paid to the beneficiary(ies) in accordance with the will.

If a testator's child is a beneficiary under the will, it is common to include a clause that determines what happens if the child predeceases the testator and is survived by his/her own child (or children)—in other words, the testator's grandchildren. If the testator wants his or her grandchildren to receive their parent's share (in the event the parent is not alive), then a **_per stirpes_** clause is included with respect to the distribution. This clause provides that the child's share will be divided equally between his or her own children (the testator's grandchildren) if the testator's child predeceases the testator. For example, assume Andrew has two sons, David and Ely. David dies before Andrew, leaving a daughter named Annie. When Andrew dies, Ely will receive 50 percent of Andrew's estate, and Annie will receive the other 50 percent. See Figure 7.1.

specific bequest
a gift of named property (including an amount of money) to a beneficiary in a will

residue
what is left of a testator's assets after the specific bequests have been distributed

liquidated
converted into cash or equivalents through sale

per stirpes
a method of distributing a gift to children pursuant to a will, which provides that if the child predeceases the testator, the child's share is divided equally among his or her children (the testator's grandchildren)

Figure 7.1   Per Stirpes Distribution: One Grandchild

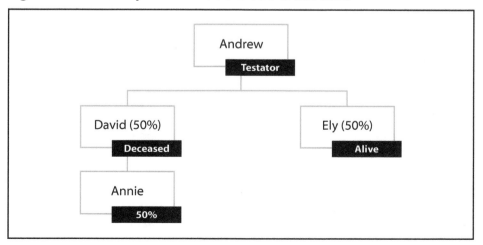

Let's continue with the above example. Now assume that both David and Ely died before Andrew. David left two children, Annie and Bram, and Ely left four children: Charles, Dina, Edward, and Frank. Annie and Bram will share equally in the 50 percent that was left to David, and therefore each receives 25 percent of Andrew's estate. Charles, Dina, Edward, and Frank will share equally in the 50 percent that was left to Ely and therefore each receives 12.5 percent of Andrew's estate. See Figure 7.2.

A person is legally entitled to receive an inheritance of money at the age of 18. Sometimes, however, a testator may want to extend this age if the testator is concerned that a particular beneficiary may not be responsible enough at 18 to deal with an inheritance of money. For example, a testator may want to leave money to his son, but wants his son to finish school or be at least 20 years old before receiving the money. In this situation, the testator can include a provision stating that the beneficiary (his son) is not entitled to receive the money until a specified time—for example, at age 21 or 25; or that the son will receive half at 21 and half at 25. The estate trustee is responsible for managing the money until it is actually paid to the beneficiary.

Figure 7.2   Per Stirpes Distribution: Multiple Grandchildren

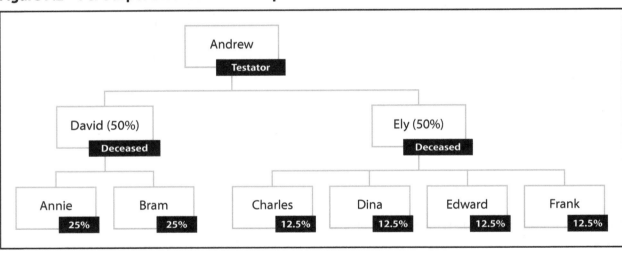

Common Disaster Clause

A common disaster clause provides that a beneficiary must outlive the testator by a certain number of days (usually 30) in order to receive the gifts made to him or her under the will. This clause is very important because it prevents an unintended or unfair distribution of the testator's estate if the testator and the beneficiary should happen to die as a result of a common accident or disaster.

The common disaster clause prevents the testator's assets from ending up with the beneficiary's beneficiaries, instead of with the testator's beneficiaries. For example, assume that Andrew and Maggie are married, and each of them has a will. Andrew has two sons by a previous relationship, and Maggie has two daughters by a previous relationship. Andrew's will leaves everything to his wife Maggie. In the event that Maggie does not survive him, he leaves everything to his two sons equally. Maggie's will leaves everything to Andrew. In the event that Andrew does not survive her, she leaves everything to her two daughters equally.

Now assume that Andrew and Maggie are involved in a car accident and that, as a result, Andrew dies instantly and Maggie dies five days later. Without a common disaster clause, Maggie will inherit everything Andrew left her, but then, after only 5 days, everything will then pass to her two daughters. This is clearly not what Andrew and Maggie would have intended. A common disaster clause prevents this unintended result from occurring. Maggie will not inherit Andrew's estate, because she did not outlive him by the required 30 days set out in the common disaster clause. Instead, Andrew's estate will go to his sons and Maggie's estate will go to her daughters, which is exactly what Andrew and Maggie intended to happen with their estates when they died.

Guardianship

When someone with young children prepares a will, he or she should state who will be the child(ren)'s **guardian** upon his/her death. A guardian is a person who takes care of the testator's minor child(ren)—that is, children under 18 years of age—in the event the testator dies. A testator may also state that the guardian shall have custody of the children upon the testator's death. However, a guardianship or custody clause in a will is not binding on the courts; it is merely a statement of the testator's intention. In other words, the person seeking custody must go to court and apply for an order granting him or her custody of the minor children. However, a guardianship clause in a will is very powerful evidence in support of the guardian's application.

> **guardian**
> a person named in a will to take care of minor children

Family Law Act Provision

A *Family Law Act* clause in a will protects beneficiaries in the event of separation or divorce.[3] For example, a father can ensure that if, after he dies, his son and daughter-in-law separate or divorce, she will not have any claim to the gift left to his son in the will. A testator does this by including a clause in the will stating that inherited property is excluded from the beneficiary's **net family property**.

Net family property is essentially the increase in value of a spouse's property from the date of the marriage to the date of separation. Property that is inherited during the marriage is typically excluded from this calculation.[4] Income from that property will also be excluded, but only if the testator specifically states this in his or her will. For example, assume that Jiava inherited $100,000 from his father during the time Jiava was married to Suzette, and he invested this money. Also assume that Jiava's father's will contained a *Family Law Act* clause excluding the income earned from any property he left to Jiava in his will. If Jiava and Suzette separate or divorce, the

> **net family property**
> the net value (value of total assets at date of separation, divorce, or death less value of assets at date of marriage) of a person's assets

---

3   RSO 1990, c. F.3.

4   Ibid., s. 4(2).

$100,000 is excluded from his net family property, as is the income Jiava earned by investing this money. If there was no *Family Law Act* clause in his father's will, Jiava would have to include in his net family property any income he earned on the $100,000 he inherited from his father. It must be noted, however, that if during his marriage Jiava puts any of his inherited money into the home he and Suzette lived in (known as the matrimonial home), that money can no longer be excluded from his net family property.

Power of Investment to Estate Trustee

A testator will usually grant very broad powers to the estate trustee named in the will. These powers include the right to invest money and the right to sell property. Basically, the estate trustee is given complete discretion to do whatever he or she deems appropriate. The testator names a particular estate trustee because the testator has complete trust in that person—this is why the estate trustee's powers are typically very broad.

Testamentary Capacity

To make a valid will, a testator must be at least 18 years old, unless the testator is or has been married. A testator who is less than 18 years old can make a will if he or she is contemplating marriage to a named person and the will is being made for that purpose. In this case, however, the will is not valid until the testator marries the named person.

To make a valid will, a testator must also have the mental capacity to understand fully what he or she is signing. The test of whether someone has this capacity is a subjective one. In other words, capacity is determined by considering whether or not the particular person who signed the will understood that what he or she signed was in fact his/her will. It is not determined by considering what a reasonable person would have understood in that situation. In other words, it is not an objective test.

If the testator is signing his/her will in the presence of the lawyer who prepared it for him/her, the lawyer may make written notes as to the client's capacity. This is especially necessary in the case of an elderly client whose mental capacity may be challenged, after his or her death, by a relative who was left out of the will or by a beneficiary who is not happy with his or her gift under the will. For example, assume Edith is 97 years old and is meeting with her lawyer to sign her will. If Edith is a very competent 97-year-old woman and fully understands what she is signing, her lawyer should make notes to that effect. These notes will carry a lot of weight in the event that Edith's daughter, who is left out of the will, challenges Edith's will when she dies.

The test of testamentary capacity was established in the 1870 case of *Bank v. Goodfellow*.[5] The court stated that to establish testamentary capacity, a person making a will must

---

5   [1870] 5 QB 549.

1. have an understanding of the nature of the activity (that is, must understand that he/she is making a will);
2. have knowledge as to the extent and nature of his/her assets;
3. have knowledge of his/her relationships and who might have an expectation to inherit; and
4. understand the impact of the will (that is, must understand who is receiving what and who is being left out).

If a person making a will satisfies all four requirements, he or she is deemed to have testamentary capacity.

Revocation

To revoke a will is to cancel or nullify it. There are several ways to revoke a will. The first way is to create a new will. A new, valid will automatically revokes an earlier will; the new will is not required to state that it revokes any previous wills. However, most wills do contain a revocation clause, stating that previous wills are revoked. If the new will is not valid, however, the former will is not revoked and it remains valid.

A will can also be revoked by the testator's physically destroying it—for example, by tearing it up or burning it.

Another way to revoke a will is by marriage. Ontario law provides that if a testator gets married after he or she executes a will, the will is revoked by the testator's marriage, unless the will was made in contemplation of the marriage.[6] For example, if Dino is planning to marry Sonya, and he signs a will that states it is being made in contemplation of his marriage to Sonya, the will remains valid after his marriage; it is not revoked. If, however, there is no mention in Dino's will of his pending marriage to Sonya, then the marriage to Sonya will revoke the will.

The reason for this automatic revocation is that it is unfair to people in Sonya's position if the testator's pre-existing will takes no account of them. At the same time, the surviving spouse need not opt for automatic revocation in the event of the testator's death. It is at his or her discretion. In other words, a married person can formally elect to receive under the will of his or her deceased spouse even if the will was not made in contemplation of marriage.

Assume that Daniel prepares a will leaving everything to his girlfriend Amanda. Five years later, Daniel and Amanda get married. In the event of Daniel's death, Amanda has the right to elect to treat Daniel's pre-marriage will as valid—which she will likely do because it is to her benefit. If she does not elect to treat the will as valid, it is automatically revoked. As stated above, the automatic revocation provision protects future spouses of the testator who might not have been considered when the will was drafted and might, therefore, not have been left anything in the event of the testator's death. In this example, however, the future spouse (Amanda) is already protected and should therefore elect to receive the entitlement under the will.

---

6 *Succession Law Reform Act*, RSO 1990, c. S.26, s. 16.

Unlike marriage, a testator's subsequent divorce does not revoke his/her will. Instead, it effectively terminates any gifts that were made to the testator's ex-spouse. If a testator gets divorced after signing his/her will, the will is interpreted as if the testator's ex-spouse predeceased the testator. For example, assume Brian prepares a will that leaves a gift to his wife Hanna. Two years later, Brian and Hanna get divorced. The will remains valid but, because Hanna is deemed to be deceased, the gift to Hanna is extinguished. It should be noted, however, that this protection applies to divorced spouses only. It does not apply to spouses who are separated.

Codicil

codicil
a legal document that amends a will

If a testator wants to make significant changes to his or her will, the best way to avoid confusion is to prepare an entirely new will. If, on the other hand, the testator wants to make only a minor change, he or she can use a **codicil**. A codicil is a document that is read in conjunction with the will it is making a minor change to. It is just as valid as the will. For example, assume that Anna has a will that names her husband as the estate trustee and her children as the beneficiaries. She now wants to leave $1,000 to her new grandson Sam. All she needs to do is prepare a codicil stating that she is leaving a $1,000 specific bequest to Sam. When Anna dies, the estate trustee will look at both the will and the codicil to determine Anna's intentions.

The formal requirements for a valid codicil are the same as those for a valid will. A codicil must be signed by the testator and witnessed by two witnesses who are both present at the same time.

Intestacy

intestate
not having a will upon death

If a person dies without a valid will, he or she is said to have died **intestate**. In the absence of a will, the *Succession Law Reform Act* governs the distribution of the estate.[7] This Act provides for the distribution of assets according to the relationship of the deceased to those relatives that survive him or her—the closest relatives of the deceased are paid out first. The basic order of lineage, which determines the order in which relatives of the deceased are paid, is as follows:

1. spouse,
2. children (and grandchildren—children of predeceased children),
3. parents,
4. siblings,
5. nieces/nephews.

---

7 RSO 1990, c. S.26.

If there are no relatives in any of the above categories, then the next of kin of equal **degree of consanguinity** to the deceased, such as grandparents and cousins, will share the amount equally. For example, if the only relatives of the deceased are two first cousins and one second cousin, the estate would be divided equally between the two first cousins. The second cousin would not receive anything. When someone dies intestate, his or her spouse is always entitled to the first $200,000 of the estate. This is known as a **preferential share**. If the estate is worth less than $200,000, the deceased's spouse will inherit the entire estate. If the deceased's estate is worth more than $200,000 and the deceased had no children, the deceased's spouse will inherit the entire estate.

If, on the other hand, the deceased died intestate and had children who survived him, the amount in excess of $200,000 is paid out as follows:

- If there is one child, the amount over $200,000 is divided equally between the spouse and the child.
- If there is more than one child, the amount over $200,000 is paid out by giving one-third to the spouse and dividing the remaining two-thirds equally between the children.

For example, assume Hasbro died intestate, was married with one child, and had an estate valued at $500,000. Hasbro's spouse will receive $350,000 ($200,000 preferential share plus one half of the balance of $300,000) and his child will receive $150,000. If, on the other hand, Hasbro had four children, his spouse will receive $300,000 ($200,000 plus one-third of the balance of $300,000) and each child will receive $50,000—two-thirds of the remaining balance of the estate ($200,000) divided equally among the four children.

If the deceased died without a spouse and without children, then the estate will go to his next of kin in the order of lineage set out above—parents, siblings, nephews/ nieces, and next of kin (grandparents, cousins). For example, if the deceased's parents survive him or her, the parents share the estate equally. If there are no parents, the siblings, if any, will share equally in the estate. If a person dies intestate and with no surviving relatives whatsoever, then the doctrine of escheat applies (discussed in Chapter 4), and all the deceased's property reverts to the Crown.

Figure 7.3 illustrates intestacy distribution.

degree of consanguinity
the closeness of legal relationships within a family

preferential share
the first $200,000 of an estate that goes to the deceased's spouse when a person dies intestate

Figure 7.3 Intestacy Distribution

Spouse only	Spouse inherits entire estate
Spouse and only one child	Spouse receives preferential share of $200,000; remainder (if any) divided equally between spouse and child
Spouse and two or more children	Spouse receives preferential share of $200,000; remainder (if any) divided as follows: 1/3 to spouse, 2/3 divided equally between children
No spouse and one or more children	Estate divided equally among children; if a child is not alive, his/her share is divided equally between his/her child(ren), if any (*per stirpes*)
No spouse and no children	Estate divided equally between grandchildren
No spouse, children, or grandchildren	Estate divided equally between parents
No spouse, children, grandchildren, or parents	Estate divided equally between brothers and sisters
No spouse, children, grandchildren, parents, or siblings	Estate divided equally between nieces and nephews
No spouse, children, grandchildren, parents, siblings, nephews, or nieces	Estate divided equally among next of kin of equal degree of consanguinity to the deceased (grandparents, cousins)
No surviving relatives	Estate reverts to the Crown

Challenging a Will

A will can be challenged or contested on several grounds. The most common reasons for challenging a will are as follows:

- The will wasn't property executed (signed and witnessed), as discussed above.
- The testator lacked testamentary capacity, as discussed above.
- There was undue influence when the testator made the will, to the extent that either there was no intent to make a will at all or the testator's true intentions are not properly conveyed in the will.

The third situation (that is, undue influence that throws into doubt the testator's intentions) renders the entire will invalid. Remember, however, that in other situations undue influence may result only in the voiding of a particular gift, not of the entire will.

As discussed earlier, a new will automatically revokes a previous will. If, however, a new will is challenged and is deemed to be invalid, the prior will continues to be legally effective. If a will is challenged and is deemed to be invalid and there is no prior will, then the deceased is deemed to have died intestate.

Family Law Act Claim

When a married person dies, there are family law rules that must be considered by his or her surviving spouse. The *Family Law Act* provides that upon the death of a spouse, the surviving spouse must elect whether to receive an **equalization of net family property** or whether to take what he or she is entitled to under the will (or, if his or her spouse died intestate, according to the distribution scheme set out in the *Succession Law Reform Act*, discussed above). A surviving spouse must make this choice within six months of his or her spouse's death. To make the right choice, a surviving spouse must determine whether the amount of the equalization of net family property will be more or less than the amount he or she is entitled to under the will or intestacy.

An equalization of net family property is a payment that reflects the difference between the net family property values of each spouse. Essentially, this means that the spouse with the higher net family property value must pay an equalization payment to the spouse with the lower net family property value in order to "equalize" their respective net family property values. For example, assume Spouse A's net family property is $180,000 and Spouse B's net family property is $100,000. Since Spouse A has the higher net family property, Spouse A will have to pay an equalization payment to Spouse B in an amount that is half of the difference between their respective net family property values. In this example, the difference is $80,000, so Spouse A must give Spouse B $40,000. They will then each have a net family property of $140,000.

Once a surviving spouse determines the amount of the net family property equalization payment he or she is entitled to, he or she can then determine whether to elect to receive this payment or whether to take what he or she is entitled to under the will (or in the case of intestacy, if there is no will).

If—to return to the above example—Spouse A died and left a will giving Spouse B $50,000, then Spouse B should elect to receive under the will because it is more than the $40,000 he or she would receive by way of an equalization payment. If, on the other hand, Spouse A's will gave Spouse B $25,000, then Spouse B should instead elect to receive the equalization payment of $40,000.

equalization of net family property
a monetary adjustment made between legally married spouses (upon separation, divorce, or death) to balance or equalize their respective net family property values

Dependant's Relief

Pursuant to Part V of the *Succession Law Reform Act*, a person who is entitled to receive support from someone who dies can claim against the deceased's estate for support if that person is not adequately provided for under the will or the intestacy rules. Support claims are typically made by the deceased's spouse or child(ren) and will be successful only if the deceased was either supporting that person or under a legal obligation to provide support to that person. For example, assume that Edna is a minor and her father pays child support for her. If her father dies and leaves Edna nothing in his will, Edna has the right to make a claim against her father's estate for child support. Similarly, if Edna's father was paying spousal support to Edna's mother (his ex-wife), her mother can also claim against the estate when Edna's father dies.

Scenario and Precedents of a Will, Affidavit of Execution, and Codicil

Scenario

Gino Green, of the City of Toronto, executed his will on January 5, year 0. He appointed his wife, Jenna Green, as his estate trustee and his sister, Samana Green, as the alternate estate trustee. Gino and Jenna have two children, ages 10 and 12. Gino is leaving everything to Jenna, and to his children, if Jenna predeceases him. He wants Samana to be the guardian of his children. Gino signed the will in front of his lawyer, Donata Brown, and Donata's law clerk, Vera Donaldson.

On June 17, year 1, Gino prepared a codicil leaving his gold Rolex watch to his sister Samana. Gino signed the codicil in the presence of the same witnesses that were the witnesses to his will.

Below are samples of the following:

- Gino's will
- affidavit of execution of Gino's will
- Gino's codicil.

WILL

THIS IS THE WILL of me, Gino Green, of the City of Toronto, and Province of Ontario, made this 5th day of January, Year 0.

I. REVOCATION

I revoke all Wills and Codicils previously made by me.

II. GUARDIAN

If my spouse predeceases me, I appoint my sister, Samana Green, to be the guardian of my children during their minority.

III. ESTATE TRUSTEE

I appoint my spouse, Jenna Green, to be the Estate Trustee of my Will. If my spouse does not survive me or is or becomes unwilling or unable to act as my Estate Trustee before all the trusts set out in my Will have been fully performed, I appoint my sister, Samana Green, to be the Estate Trustee of my Will.

IV. TRANSFERS TO ESTATE TRUSTEE

I give all my property to my Estate Trustee upon the following trusts:

1. PERSONAL PROPERTY

1.1 My Estate Trustee shall deliver to my spouse, Jenna Green, if she is living on the thirtieth day following the date of my death, all articles of personal and household use or ornament, and all automobiles and their accessories.

1.2 If my spouse is not then living, my Estate Trustee shall deliver to my children all articles of personal and household use or ornament, and all automobiles and their accessories. Any articles not delivered shall fall into the residue of my estate.

1.3 Any articles not distributed or retained shall become part of the residue of my estate.

2. DEBTS AND DEATH TAXES

My Estate Trustee shall pay out of the capital of my estate all my just debts, including any income taxes payable for the year(s) prior to my death and in the year of my death to the date of my death, funeral and testamentary expenses, and all succession duties, estate, gift, inheritance and death taxes, whether imposed pursuant to the law of this or any other jurisdiction, otherwise payable by any beneficiary under my Will or any Codicil or of any settlement made by me, by any beneficiary named by me in any insurance policy, plan or contract owned by me, or by any donee of any gift made by me.

3. CONVERSION OF MY ASSETS

My Estate Trustee shall call in the assets of my estate and may sell the assets at such times, for such price, in such manner and upon such terms as my Estate Trustee in the exercise of an absolute discretion considers appropriate.

I authorize my Estate Trustee to hold any asset of my estate without liability for loss or depreciation for as long as my Estate Trustee in the exercise of an absolute discretion considers appropriate, whether or not it may not be an investment in which a trustee may by law invest trust funds.

4. RESIDUE

If my spouse, Jenna Green, is living on the thirtieth day following the date of my death, my Estate Trustee shall pay and transfer the residue of my estate to my spouse for her own use absolutely.

5. ALTERNATE RESIDUE

If my spouse is not living on the thirtieth day following the date of my death, my Estate Trustee shall divide the residue of my estate into a number of equal parts so that there is one part for each of the children living at the date of my death and one part for each of the children not then living with issue then living, and divide the part of the child not then living among the then living issue of such child in equal shares per stirpes.

V. POWERS OF ESTATE TRUSTEE

In order to carry out the trusts of my Will, I give my Estate Trustee the following powers to be used in the exercise of an absolute discretion at any time:

1. INVESTMENTS

My Estate Trustee shall make any investments for my estate that my Estate Trustee considers appropriate, including units or other interests of any mutual funds, common trust funds, unit trusts or similar investments, without being limited to those investments authorized by law for trustees. My Estate Trustee shall not be liable for any loss that may happen to my estate as a result of any investment made by my Estate Trustee in good faith.

2. SELLING AND DISPOSING

My Estate Trustee shall realize or dispose of the assets of my estate, in any manner and on any terms.

3. RETENTION OF ASSETS

My Estate Trustee shall hold any of my assets in the form in which they may be at the time of my death for any length of time, whether or not they might not be assets in which trustees would otherwise be entitled to invest trust moneys. Those assets so retained shall be deemed to be authorized investments.

4. DISTRIBUTION IN SPECIE

My Estate Trustee shall make any division, distribution or allocation of the assets of my estate in kind and at such valuations as my Estate Trustee in the exercise of an absolute discretion considers appropriate. In determining such valuations, my Estate Trustee may consider such future expectations for such assets as my Estate Trustee in the exercise of an absolute discretion considers appropriate, including any tax liability or credit. Any decision of my Estate Trustee in this regard shall be binding on all persons concerned.

VI. DEFINITION OF RELATIONSHIPS

Any reference in my Will to a person in terms of a relationship to another person determined by blood or marriage shall not include a person born outside marriage or a person who comes within the description traced through another person who was born outside marriage. Any person who has been legally adopted shall be regarded as having been born in the marriage of his or her adopting parent.

VII. EXCLUSIONS FROM NET FAMILY PROPERTY

I declare that the income, including capital gains, arising from any interest passing to a beneficiary under my Will shall be excluded from such beneficiary's net family property or from the value of the beneficiary's assets on the death, divorce or separation of such beneficiary, pursuant to the *Family Law Act*, R.S.O. 1990, c. F.3.

All gifts made to a beneficiary shall be the separate property of my beneficiaries and shall not fall into any Community of Property or be subject to any other matrimonial rights of the spouses of my beneficiaries and shall not be liable for the obligations of any such spouses or Community. All such gifts shall not be subject to seizure for the payment of any debts of beneficiaries or their representatives while in the possession and control of my Estate Trustee.

VIII. COMPENSATION

I authorize my Estate Trustee to take and transfer at reasonable intervals from the income and/or capital of my estate amounts on account of his or her compensation which my Estate Trustee reasonably anticipates will be requested at the end of the accounting period in progress, either upon the audit of the estate accounts or on approval by the beneficiaries of my estate. If the amount subsequently awarded on Court audit or agreed to by the beneficiaries is less than the amount so taken, the excess shall be repaid to my estate without interest.

IX. GOVERNING LAW

My Will shall be governed by and construed in accordance with the laws of the Province of Ontario.

IN TESTIMONY WHEREOF I have to my Will, which is written upon this and the 4 preceding pages of paper, subscribed my name on the day and year first above written.

SIGNED by GINO GREEN,
as his will, in the presence
of us both, present at the same
time, who at his request, in his
presence and in the presence of   _____
each other have   GINO GREEN
subscribed our names as witnesses:

1. _____
    Signature of witness
    Print name: Donata Brown
    Address:
    Occupation: Lawyer

2. _____
    Signature of witness
    Print name: Vera Donaldson
    Address:
    Occupation: Law Clerk

AFFIDAVIT OF EXECUTION
ONTARIO SUPERIOR COURT
AFFIDAVIT OF EXECUTION OF WILL

IN THE MATTER OF THE WILL OF GINO GREEN

I, Donata Brown, of the City of Toronto, and Province of Ontario, make oath and say:

1) On or about the 5th day of January Year 0, I was present and saw the paper writing annexed and marked as Exhibit "A" to this my Affidavit executed by Gino Green.

2) At the time of execution, I knew such person, who was on that date of the full age of eighteen years to the best of my knowledge.

3) The said paper writing was executed by such person in the presence of Vera Donaldson, of the City of Toronto and Province of Ontario, and me, and we were both present at the same time, whereupon we did, in the presence of such person, attest and subscribe the said paper writing as witnesses.

SWORN before me at the   )
City of Toronto   )
and Province of   )   _____
Ontario, this 5th day of   )   ~~GINO GREEN~~ Donata Brown
January, Year 0   )
A Commissioner for Oaths, etc.

CODICIL

THIS IS A FIRST CODICIL to the Will of me, Gino Green, of the City of Toronto, and Province of Ontario, which Will is dated the 5th day of January, Year 0.

1. I declare that the following Paragraph shall be inserted after Paragraph 1, Personal Property, and shall have the same effect as if it had been originally inserted therein.

1.1 My Estate Trustee shall deliver to my sister, Samana Green, my gold Rolex watch.

2. In all other respects, I confirm my Will.

IN TESTIMONY WHEREOF I have to this first Codicil to my Will, which is written upon this page of paper, subscribed my name on the 17th day of June, Year 1

SIGNED BY GINO GREEN	)
as a First Codicil to his Will, in the presence	)
of us both, present at the same time, who at his	)
request, and in his presence and in the presence	)
of each other have subscribed our names as	)
witnesses:	

GINO GREEN

1. _____
    Signature of Witness:
    Name and Address
    Donata Brown

2. _____
    Signature of Witness:
    Name and Address
    Vera Donaldson

KEY TERMS

affidavit of execution, 101
beneficiary, 100
codicil, 108
degree of consanguinity, 109
equalization of net family property, 111
estate, 100
estate trustee, 100

executed, 100
guardian, 105
holograph will, 101
intestate, 108
liquidated, 103
net family property, 105
per stirpes, 103

preferential share, 109
residue, 103
specific bequest, 103
testamentary intent, 101
testator, 100
undue influence, 100
will/last will and testament, 100

REVIEW QUESTIONS

1. What are the formal requirements of a valid will?

2. Giuseppe recently died and his children found a document that states how he wants his estate distributed. The document is signed by Giuseppe but is handwritten by him. Is this a valid will and, if so, what type of will is it?

3. Sandrina died, and in her will she left her car to Donna and everything else to Edna. Who are the beneficiaries of Sandrina's estate? Who is the beneficiary of the residue of Sandrina's estate?

4. Wilma's will leaves everything to her three daughters equally, and it provides that in the event that a child predeceases her, the estate is to be distributed *per stirpes*. Wilma's daughter, Georgina, predeceased Wilma but is survived by her two sons (Wilma's grandsons). How will Wilma's estate be distributed?

5. What do we call the person who is named in a will to take care of minor children?

6. Joshua signed his will several years ago and now wants to make a minor change to it. What document does Joshua need to prepare?

7. What is dying without a valid will called?

8. Janice has a will that was executed while she was married to Bruno. In the will, she leaves Bruno her 1960 Corvette. Janice and Bruno are now divorced. When Janice dies, will Bruno inherit the 1960 Corvette? Explain your answer.

9. Francoise died intestate, and she is survived by her husband Georges and their daughter Monique. Francoise's estate is worth $350,000. How will her estate be distributed?

10. Dominique recently died, leaving his wife Annalise. His net family property was $200,000 and Annalise's net family property was $100,000. Dominique's will leaves Annalise a gift of $100,000. Should Annalise elect to take her gift under the will or to receive an equalization payment? Explain your answer.

[handwritten notes:]

1. It must be properly sign by a testator and must have withness.

2. Yes it is a Va

Estate Administration

LEARNING OUTCOMES

After reading this chapter, you should be able to:

- Understand the meaning of estate administration

- Describe the difference between administering an estate with a will and administering an estate without a will

- Explain the purpose of a Certificate of Appointment of Estate Trustee

- Understand the responsibilities of an estate trustee

- Understand the tax that must be paid in order to obtain a certificate of appointment, and how to calculate the tax

- Describe the compensation that may be paid to an estate trustee

- Explain what happens when gifts in a will are not possible owing to insufficiency in the estate

Introduction

Estate administration is the process that a person undertakes when distributing the estate of a deceased person. If the deceased had a valid will, estate administration involves carrying out his or her wishes as stated in the will. If, on the other hand, the deceased person died intestate (without a valid will), estate administration involves distributing his or her estate in accordance with the intestacy rules discussed in Chapter 7. In short, the estate of every deceased person must be administered, regardless of whether or not the deceased had a valid will.

As discussed in Chapter 7, the person who administers an estate is called the estate trustee. If the deceased had a will, the estate trustee (formerly called the executor) is the person(s) named in the will who is authorized to administer the estate. However, depending on the circumstances, the estate trustee may need to apply to the court for a **Certificate of Appointment of Estate Trustee With a Will** (also known as "letters probate") in order to deal with the deceased's property. This certificate proves that the court has validated the deceased's will, and it confirms the estate trustee's authority to administer the deceased's estate. If someone dies without a will, the person who wants to act as the estate trustee must apply to the court for a **Certificate of Appointment of Estate Trustee Without a Will** (also known as "letters of administration"). Because the proposed estate trustee is not deriving his or her power from a will, he or she must obtain the court's permission to act as the estate trustee (formerly called an administrator) and to administer the deceased's estate. A person who applies to be appointed as the estate trustee must prove that he or she has the beneficiaries' consent (discussed below).

Certificate of Appointment of Estate Trustee With a Will

The estate trustee(s) who is named in a testator's will has the power to administer the deceased's estate. However, in many if not most cases, a Certificate of Appointment of Estate Trustee With a Will is also required as further proof of the estate trustee's authority. For example, a third party who deals with the estate trustee, such as a bank, will likely require this further assurance before releasing any money to an estate trustee.

Also, if the testator owned real property registered in the Land Titles System, the estate trustee cannot transfer title to a beneficiary or purchaser without first obtaining a Certificate of Appointment of Estate Trustee With a Will.

The process of applying for a Certificate of Appointment of Estate Trustee With a Will still often involves the traditional legal terms "probate" and "probating a will." **Probate** is the court process by which a will is proved valid or invalid. There are some situations where probate is not necessary, and in these situations a certificate is not required. Where possible, an estate trustee should avoid probate because, as discussed below, probate can be a costly and time-consuming process.

Each estate is different. Whether an estate trustee can proceed without obtaining a certificate will depend on the particular circumstances. There are some transactions involving real property that an estate trustee can conduct without having to obtain a certificate of appointment. The following are some examples of these transactions:

- When dealing with real property that is registered in the Registry System, the estate trustee does not need a certificate of appointment.

- If the property was originally in the Registry System and was converted to the Land Titles System, and the transfer by the estate trustee is the first transaction since the date of conversion—known as a **first dealing**—then a certificate of appointment is not required. However, if the property being transferred is registered in the Land Titles System, an estate trustee does need to obtain a certificate of appointment.

- If the estate trustee is dealing with real property that the deceased owned as a joint tenant, a certificate of appointment is not required. As discussed in Chapter 4, when a person owns property as a joint tenant, title to that property will automatically vest in the surviving joint tenant(s) when that person dies (by the principle known as the right of survivorship). The property, in this case, never even becomes part of the deceased's estate, and probate (and obtaining a certificate of appointment) is therefore not required.

first dealing
the first transaction after property is converted from the Registry System to the Land Titles System

Whether a certificate of appointment is required in a case where there is no real property will depend on the value of the deceased's assets and on where these assets are held. Typically, the higher the value of the assets, the more likely it is that the estate will have to be probated. This is because a third party, such as a bank, is more likely to insist on the certificate when it is holding a considerable amount of money and is thereby assuming more risk.

For example, assume that Frederick died with a will. A bank releases money to the estate trustee without insisting that Frederick's estate be probated. In other words, the bank does not require a Certificate of Appointment of Estate Trustee With a Will. Assume also that Sam is a beneficiary under Frederick's will and has not been paid his inheritance in accordance with the terms of that will. If it turns out that there is not enough money left in the estate to pay Sam, he may have a claim against the bank for releasing money to the estate trustee without probating Frederick's estate. As this example shows, the greater the potential claim against an estate, the greater the bank's risk in not insisting that the estate be probated before releasing funds to an estate trustee.

Whether the estate will be probated also depends on what bank the deceased's assets are being held in. Some banks insist on probate while others are more lenient. The bank's decision in this regard may be influenced by its prior relationship with the testator. For example, if the testator was a longstanding customer and the bank knew the testator's family, the bank may be more comfortable releasing the testator's savings without the need for probate. Whoever has control of the deceased's assets must decide, before distributing the assets to the estate trustee, whether or not a certificate of appointment is required. In other words, there is no legal requirement to receive a certificate of appointment before releasing the assets; the holder of the assets has the discretion to make this decision based on the nature and value of the assets and/or on the relationship the holder has with the deceased and his/her family.

It should be noted that if the deceased had multiple assets at different institutions, then probate is required as soon as one of the institutions insists on it. For example, assume Michael died testate, and his estate was not probated (in other words, the estate trustee did not obtain a Certificate of Appointment of Estate Trustee With a Will). Michael had stocks with Trader Company, and bank accounts at both Friendly Bank and Happy Bank. Both banks are willing to release funds without a certificate of appointment, but Trader Company is not. Even though only one of the institutions insists on probate, Michael's entire estate must be probated. As a result, an **estate administration tax**, discussed below, will have to be paid on the entire estate, which includes all of the deceased's assets.

If the certificate of appointment is required, the estate trustee, through a lawyer, applies for it by filing numerous documents with the court, including the original will, the codicil(s) if any, and the affidavit of execution. The estate trustee must also pay the estate administration tax upon filing these documents. The amount of this tax is based on the value of the estate. The documents will also include proof that notice of the application for the certificate of appointment has been served on all of the beneficiaries under the testator's will. Once the court issues the certificate of appointment, the estate trustee can begin distributing the deceased's estate in accordance with the will.

estate administration tax
the tax that is paid when an estate is probated

Certificate of Appointment of Estate Trustee Without a Will

If a person dies intestate, someone must apply to the court to obtain a Certificate of Appointment of Estate Trustee Without a Will in order to be given the power to administer the deceased's estate. Once the certificate is granted, the applicant will become the estate trustee. Generally speaking, a certificate of appointment becomes less avoidable when someone dies intestate. Without a will, there is no proof at all of the person's authority to act on behalf of the estate. And without any evidence of the deceased's intentions, the asset holder will be extremely reluctant to release assets to anyone without a certificate of appointment.

In order to apply for the Certificate of Appointment of Estate Trustee Without a Will, the applicant must have the consent of the beneficiaries who represent a majority of interest in the estate. For example, if the deceased is survived by three children and no spouse, two of the children will represent a majority of interest in the estate; the laws of intestacy state that the three children are each entitled to one-third of the estate.

The proposed estate trustee must file similar forms to those that are filed when there is a will, though in this case, of course, there is not an actual will, codicil, or affidavit of execution to file with the court. The applicant must also file an affidavit of service to all beneficiaries of the deceased's estate, as determined by the laws of intestacy.

In addition, the person who is applying to be the estate trustee must provide an **administration bond of indemnity** to the court, together with instructions to release those funds in the event of impropriety. The bond protects the beneficiaries and creditors of the estate while the estate trustee is administering it. Because the estate trustee will have full control over the deceased's assets, the bond gives an assurance to the court that the estate trustee will distribute the estate properly. The bond instructs a third party, usually a bank, to compensate any party who has proven that he or she has suffered a loss as a result of the estate trustee's improper actions. For example, if the estate trustee left out one of the children of the deceased when distributing the estate, and the child proved his or her entitlement under intestacy law, the bond would act as the authority to the third party, such as a bank, to pay the money owing to the child from the funds that are posted in the bond.

In some cases, the estate trustee does not need to post a bond. For example, if the applicant is the spouse of the deceased and the size of the estate is less than $200,000, a bond is not required. This is because, as explained in Chapter 7, when a person dies intestate, his/her surviving spouse is entitled to the first $200,000 of the estate (that is, the preferential share). If the applicant is the surviving spouse, then he or she is the sole beneficiary of the deceased's estate. It is therefore not possible to leave an entitled beneficiary out of the estate. If the applicant is not the spouse of the deceased but is the sole beneficiary of the deceased's estate, a bond is not required, either. For example, assume the deceased died without a will and had no spouse and only one child. In this situation, the only person entitled to the estate under the intestacy rules set out in the *Succession Law Reform Act*[1] is the deceased's child. Because no one can be jeopardized by the administration of the estate, the child will likely not have to post a bond when he or she applies for a Certificate of Appointment of Estate Trustee Without a Will.

Once a Certificate of Appointment of Estate Trustee Without a Will is granted, the estate trustee will have the power to distribute the estate in accordance with the *Succession Law Reform Act*.

Estate Administration Tax

The estate trustee must pay a tax when applying for a Certificate of Appointment of Estate Trustee (with or without a will). This tax is called an estate administration tax and is commonly referred to as **probate fees**. Except in rare circumstances (which are beyond the scope of this book), as when the testator had multiple wills, the estate administration tax must be paid on the total value of the entire estate. For example, if Morgan's estate includes a car valued at $5,000, a house valued at $200,000, and a bank account with $25,000, the tax will be paid on $230,000, which is the total value of the estate.

administration bond of indemnity
money that is secured with a third party and paid out in the event that the estate trustee does not pay a person entitled to be paid from the estate

probate fees
an estate administration tax; the estate trustee must pay this tax when applying for a Certificate of Appointment of Estate Trustee (with or without a will)

---

1 RSO 1990, c. S.26.

The values of any assets that pass directly to the beneficiaries (without going through the estate) are not included in the calculation of this tax. Because of the tax savings, it is always an advantage when property can pass to beneficiaries without going through the estate. Some examples of property that can pass to a beneficiary without going through the estate are the following:

1. *Life insurance policies that have named beneficiaries.* For example, if Morgan, when he died, had a life insurance policy in the amount of $100,000, and the policy named his spouse, Candice, as the beneficiary, the policy's value—$100,000—will not be included in the total value of the estate when the tax is calculated.

2. *Real property that is held by joint tenants.* Property that is owned by two or more people as joint tenants automatically passes to the surviving joint tenant(s). If the property is registered in the Land Titles System, the only thing that must be done to transfer legal title from both joint tenants to the surviving joint tenant is for the latter to register a **survivorship application** on title to the property. A survivorship application contains the information about the death of a joint tenant in affidavit form, and it thereby proves that the joint tenant has died. In the Registry System, it is even easier to transfer property to the surviving joint tenant(s). In this system, only a death certificate must be registered on title. If, in the above example, Morgan and his wife owned their house as joint tenants, the value of the house ($200,000) would not be included when calculating the estate administration tax. The value of the estate for tax purposes would therefore be only $30,000.

3. *Joint bank accounts.* If the deceased had a bank account that was held jointly with another person, the account passes to that other person without going through the deceased's estate. For example, if Morgan and Candice had savings of $25,000 in a joint bank account when Morgan died, Candice will be entitled to keep the entire amount, and Morgan's amount will not be included in the value of the estate when the estate administration tax is calculated.

Estate administration tax is paid as follows:

- on the first $50,000 of the estate, at the rate of .5 percent;
- on the balance of the estate, at the rate of 1.5 percent.

For example, if Morgan's estate is valued at $230,000, the estate administration tax would be $2,950, calculated as follows:

- .5 percent of $50,000 = $250 ($50,000 × .005) and
- 1.5 percent of the balance (230,000 − 50,000 = 180,000) = $2,700 ($180,000 × .015).

survivorship application
the document that gets registered on title to prove the right of survivorship in a joint tenancy

Distribution of Estate

The estate trustee is responsible for distributing the estate, either in accordance with the will, if there is one, or pursuant to the *Succession Law Reform Act*, if the person died intestate.

The first thing that the estate trustee must do is pay any **creditors** of the estate. Creditors of an estate typically include credit card companies, banks (for the payment of a loan or mortgage), and the government (for unpaid income tax). After all debts have been paid, the estate can be distributed. If someone dies intestate, his or her estate is distributed in accordance with the intestacy rules set out in the *Succession Law Reform Act* (as discussed in Chapter 7). If there is a will, the estate is distributed in accordance with the terms of the will.

A problem may arise if the testator's estate does not contain all of the assets that are mentioned in his or her will. For instance, a testator's will may leave a specific gift to a beneficiary which, at the time of the testator's death, no longer exists. If this happens, the missing gift fails; that is, it cannot be fulfilled. For example, assume that Kerk left in his will a valuable piece of art to Marissa, but then sold the art before he died. Since the art is no longer part of Kerk's estate when he dies, the gift to Marissa fails. This principle is called **ademption**.

Gifts fail according to a prescribed order. In other words, if the testator's estate does not contain all of the assets mentioned in the will, the gifts will fail in the following order:

1. *The residue.* As discussed in Chapter 7, the **residue of the estate** is everything that is left over after debts have been paid and specific gifts have been distributed. If there is nothing remaining in the estate after these things have been distributed, there is no residue. For example, if the testator left his car to his brother and the rest of his estate to charity, the entire estate, other than the car, is the residue. It may turn out that there is no money in the estate after all debts are paid. In this case, the charity will not receive anything.

2. *General legacies.* A **general legacy** is an amount of money with no named source. For example, "I leave $10,000 to my sister." The amount is stated but the source of the money is not.

3. *Demonstrative legacies.* A **demonstrative legacy** is an amount of money with a named source. For example, "I leave $10,000 to my sister from my bank account at Data Bank of Canada, account #45672."

4. *Specific legacies.* A **specific legacy** is the gift of a specific item. For example, "I leave my gold watch to my cousin Amelia Watt."

5. *Devises.* A **devise** is the gift of real property. For example, "I leave my house to my daughter."

Let's consider the following example. Bari's will states the following: "I leave my house to my daughter, my watch to my son, my car to my mother, $20,000 from account #9643 at ABC Bank to my brother, $30,000 to my sister, and the residue of my estate to my son and daughter equally." The estate assets and their distribution in Bari's will are as shown in Figures 8.1 and 8.2.

creditor
a party to whom money is owed

ademption
the failing of a gift that no longer exists

residue of the estate
everything that is left over after debts have been paid and specific gifts have been distributed

general legacy
an amount of money to be paid from the estate without mentioning a particular source

demonstrative legacy
an amount of money to be paid from the estate from a particular source

specific legacy
a gift of a specific item

devise
a gift of real property

Figure 8.1   Bari's Estate

Asset	Beneficiary	Description
House	Daughter	Devise
Watch	Son	Specific Legacy
Car	Mother	Specific Legacy
$20,000 in Account #9643 at ABC Bank	Brother	Demonstrative Legacy
$30,000	Sister	General Legacy
Balance of Estate	Son and Daughter	Residue

Figure 8.2   Distribution of Bari's Will

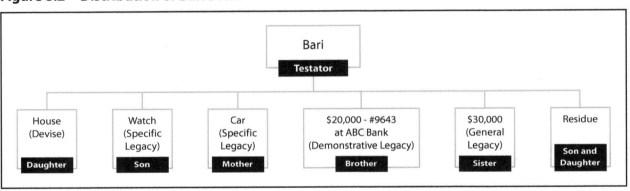

Assume that when Bari dies, he still owns the house, watch, and car, and has $100,000 in bank account #9643 at ABC Bank. All of the gifts will succeed. In other words, the house, watch, car, demonstrative legacy ($20,000), and general legacy ($30,000) can all be distributed to their chosen beneficiaries. The sum of $50,000 ($100,000 minus $20,000 minus $30,000) that is left over forms the residue of the estate, to be paid to his son and daughter equally. (See Figure 8.3.)

Figure 8.3   Residue of Bari's Estate

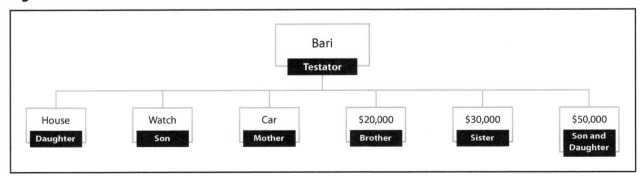

If, when he died, Bari still owned all of the items (house, watch, and car) but had only $30,000 in account #9643, there will be no residue in the estate. (See Figure 8.4.) The demonstrative legacy of $20,000 is paid in full, and the remaining $10,000 goes toward the general legacy of $30,000. Because there is not enough money to pay the full amount of the general legacy, it will be reduced to $10,000. This is known as **abatement**—the reduction of a gift when there is not enough money in the estate to pay it in its entirety. If there were a demonstrative legacy of $20,000 and two general legacies each in the amount of $30,000, the general legacies will be reduced, or abated, proportionately. The two beneficiaries will share the available funds equally; each will receive $5,000.

abatement
the reduction of a gift when there is not enough money in the estate to pay the entire gift

Figure 8.4   No Residue

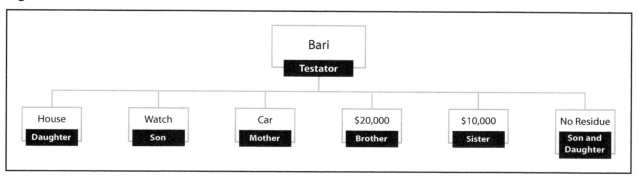

Now assume that Bari, at his death, owns all assets except the watch and has only $15,000 in account #9643 at ABC Bank. In this case, there is no residue; the specific legacy fails; the general legacy fails; and the demonstrative legacy—the gift to his brother—abates to $15,000. (See Figure 8.5.) If the full demonstrative gift is not available, it will abate. This is because bank account #9643 at ABC Bank was specifically mentioned in Bari's will, and therefore the amount must be paid from that account only. If Bari's will had said, "$20,000 from my bank account #9643 at ABC Bank or from any other account with available funds" and Bari had another bank account with at least $5,000 in it, Bari's brother would receive the full amount of $20,000, notwithstanding the shortfall in bank account #9643.

Figure 8.5   No Residue, Failure of Specific and General Legacies, and Abatement

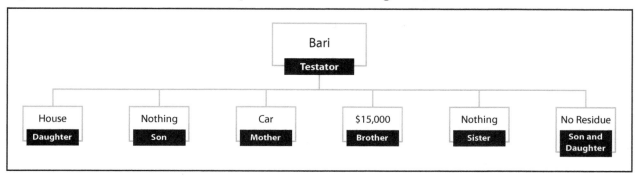

As with general legacies, if there is more than one demonstrative legacy from the same source and the source is insufficient to cover both, they will abate proportionately. For example, if Bari's will left $20,000 from bank account #9643 at ABC Bank to Bari's best friend as well as the $20,000 to Bari's brother, the two demonstrative legacies will abate together. Each beneficiary will receive $7,500 (50 percent of $15,000). A demonstrative legacy will sometimes be interpreted as a general legacy if the location of the demonstrative gift no longer exists at all. For example, if Bari had $100,000 in the bank when he died but switched bank accounts and no longer had account #9643 at ABC Bank, the court may interpret the demonstrative legacy of $20,000 as a general legacy and pay his brother the amount out of an existing bank account together with other general legacies.

Specific legacies such as the car and watch will be paid out if they exist. If they do not exist, the gift will fail. For example, if Bari no longer owns the watch, Bari's son will not receive anything—he will not receive money in lieu of the watch because the intent in the will is to give his son the watch, not the value of the watch. This is based on the principle of ademption, discussed above, and occurs when a specific gift does not exist at the time of the testator's death and cannot therefore be distributed to the beneficiary.

The last gift to fail is a devise, or real property. As long as the real property exists at the time of death, the beneficiary will receive the real property, less the value of any debts (that is, mortgages registered against the land).

lapse
what happens to a gift when the beneficiary predeceases the testator

A gift will **lapse** if the beneficiary is not alive to receive it. For example, if Bari's mother passed away before Bari, and Bari did not name an alternate beneficiary for the car, the gift of the car will lapse and will be added to the residue of the estate.

A summary of the principles of ademption and abatement is provided in Figure 8.6.

Figure 8.6   Estate Administration—Summary of Principles of Ademption and Abatement

Order of Ademption	Nature of Gift	Explanation	Example	Effect of Ademption and Abatement
1	Residue of estate	What remains after all debts/expenses have been paid and all gifts distributed	"I leave my house to my wife, and *the rest of my estate to my son Gregory*"	Gift fails if nothing is left in the estate—no residue
2	General legacy	Monetary gift with no source specified	"I leave $25,000 to my son Gregory"	• Gift abates if not enough money in the estate to pay full amount • Gift fails if no money is left after paying demonstrative legacies
3	Demonstrative legacy	Monetary gift with a source specified	"I leave $25,000 in account #12345 at Friendly Bank to my son Gregory"	• Gift abates if less than $25,000 in account #12345 • Gift fails if $0 in account #12345 (but may be treated as a general legacy)

Order of Ademption	Nature of Gift	Explanation	Example	Effect of Ademption and Abatement
4	Specific legacy	Gift of a specific asset	"I leave my gold Rolex watch to my son Gregory"	Gift fails if the gold Rolex watch no longer exists, even if the deceased owned other watches
			"I leave my watch to my son Gregory"	Gift fails if the deceased did not own a watch
5	Devise	Gift of real property	"I leave my house at 123 Anywhere Street to my son Gregory"	Gift fails if the house at 123 Anywhere Street was sold before death, even if another house is part of the estate
			"I leave my house to my son Gregory"	Gift fails if the deceased did not own a house

Note: A gift lapses if a beneficiary is not alive to receive it.

Compensation to Estate Trustee

An estate trustee is entitled to be compensated for his or her work in administering and distributing the estate. The amount is typically calculated as 2.5 percent of the assets coming into the estate and 2.5 percent of the assets that are distributed. If the estate trustee is also a beneficiary, the value of the estate for the purpose of calculating the compensation will be reduced by the value of the gift going to the estate trustee. For example, if the testator leaves an estate valued at $300,000 and a gift of $100,000 is left to the estate trustee, the latter's compensation will be calculated by using the amount of $200,000 as the amount to be distributed.

Sometimes the estate trustee's compensation can be approved informally, if the residual beneficiaries do not object. In some cases, there may have to be a more formal accounting process, known as the **passing of accounts**. This requires the estate trustee to present his or her accounts to the beneficiaries and the court. The accounts are examined by the court, in detail, to determine if the estate trustee's compensation is reasonable. If so, the account is approved or "passed" by the court. If not, the court can amend the account before approving it or not allow it at all if the estate trustee did not administer the estate properly.

passing of accounts
the formal process required in order to justify the estate trustee's compensation

KEY TERMS

abatement, 127
ademption, 125
administration bond of indemnity, 123
Certificate of Appointment of Estate Trustee
 With a Will, 120
Certificate of Appointment of Estate Trustee
 Without a Will, 120
creditor, 125
demonstrative legacy, 125
devise, 125

estate administration tax, 122
first dealing, 121
general legacy, 125
lapse, 128
passing of accounts, 129
probate fees, 123
probate/probated, 120
residue of the estate, 125
specific legacy, 125
survivorship application, 124

REVIEW QUESTIONS

1. What is the purpose of probating a will?

2. For the following transactions, state whether or not the estate trustee must obtain a Certificate of Appointment of Estate Trustee:

   a. transferring title to property registered in the Registry System.

   b. transferring title to property that has always been registered in the Land Titles System.

   c. transferring title to property that was recently converted from the Registry System to the Land Titles System under circumstances where this is the first transaction since the date of conversion.

3. Jorge recently died, and his will names Soonyi as the estate trustee of Jorge's estate. Jorges and his partner Manuel owned real property as joint tenants. Is Soonyi required to probate Jorge's will in order to deal with the real property?

4. Sancho died, leaving a considerable amount of money in his savings account at Friendly Bank. Sancho opened this bank account about six months before he died and did most of his banking online. The bank has never met Sancho's family. Discuss whether or not the bank is likely to require a Certificate of Appointment of Estate Trustee before releasing the funds in Sancho's account.

5. What is an administration bond of indemnity?

6. How are probate fees calculated?

7. Silvano's estate includes the following assets: a car valued at $10,000; a $500,000 life insurance policy naming his spouse as the beneficiary; a home registered in his name, valued at $500,000; and $50,000 cash. What is the value of the estate for the purpose of calculating the estate administration tax? Explain your answer.

8. Amanda died, and her will leaves her motorcycle to her boyfriend, Pablo, and her car to her sister, Beatrice. A year before Amanda died, she was in an accident that completely destroyed her motorcycle. Beatrice died six months ago. Explain what happens to the gifts to Pablo and Beatrice.

9. Vinny and Stano own, as joint tenants, a condominium that is registered in the Land Titles system. Vinny recently passed away. What must be done to transfer legal title of the property from Vinny and Stano to Stano only?

10. Wilma died, and her will provides that each of her two sisters is to receive $10,000, payable from bank account #4567 at ABC Bank. At the time of Wilma's death, there was only $15,000 in that account. How much will each sister receive? Explain your answer.

Powers of Attorney 9

LEARNING OUTCOMES

After reading this chapter, you should be able to:

- Understand the concept of a power of attorney and describe how a power of attorney is created

- Explain when a power of attorney becomes effective and when it ends

- Explain the differences between a power of attorney for property and a power of attorney for personal care, and identify the scope of each type of power of attorney

- Understand the legal requirements of the grantor and of the attorney

- Understand the concept of mental incapacity

- Describe how to revoke a power of attorney

Introduction

incapacity

incapacity
inability to understand
essential information
necessary to make a
particular personal care or
property-related decision
or to appreciate the
implications of making
a specific decision or of
making no decision

power of attorney
a document that provides
legal authorization to act
on behalf of someone
else and to make binding
decisions for him/her

attorney
the person who is named
or appointed to act on
behalf of someone else
(in a power of attorney)

jointly
together; the term applied
to an arrangement whereby
multiple attorneys cannot
act independently

jointly and severally
the term applied to an
arrangement whereby
multiple attorneys can
make decisions separately,
independent of each other

**power of attorney
for property**
provides legal authorization
to act on someone's behalf
and make binding decisions
for him or her about
property and finances

**power of attorney for
personal care**
provides legal authorization
to act on someone's behalf
and make binding personal
care decisions for him or her

In Chapter 7, we talked about how people can plan ahead and deal with what will happen to all of their property when they die. Having a valid will ensures that all personal and real property owned upon death will be distributed according to the deceased person's wishes.

Death is a certainty that everyone can prepare for by having a will. Sometimes, however, owing to serious mental or physical illness, people become incapable of making decisions about their property before they die. In this situation, a will is not the answer. In another case, a person may know that he or she will be unable to sign legal documents because he or she will be out of the country for an extended period of time or otherwise unavailable. A person in this situation may want to plan ahead and authorize another person to sign on his/her behalf. This chapter focuses on how people can prepare for the possibility that at some point they may become unable to make decisions and manage their personal and/or financial affairs.

The *Substitute Decisions Act*[1] is the Ontario statute that governs what happens when someone is not able to make decisions for him/herself. It regulates the process of planning ahead not for death but for **incapacity** or unavailability, through a legal document called a **power of attorney**. What is a power of attorney? When you create a power of attorney, you are giving someone else—someone you trust—the authority to act on your behalf and make binding decisions for you about your property, your finances, or even your personal care should you become either incapable of making these types of decisions yourself or simply unavailable (in the case of property). The person you appoint to take care of your affairs is called an **attorney**. The word "attorney" does not mean the person has to be a lawyer. You can choose a friend, a relative, or anyone else to be the attorney, provided he or she meets the minimum age requirements set out in the legislation (discussed below). The attorney can be the person whom you name as the estate trustee in your will, or it can be someone different.

A power of attorney is effective only while you are still alive and is therefore completely separate from a will. The person you choose as your attorney should be someone who is responsible, reliable, and absolutely trustworthy. Your attorney will be making very important decisions on your behalf and will have complete access to your money and other property (subject to any limitations stated in the power of attorney). You may name more than one attorney, in which case you must state whether you want the attorneys to act **jointly** (in which case they must make all decisions together), or **jointly and severally** (in which case they may make decisions independently).

The two main types of powers of attorney in Ontario are the following:

- a **power of attorney for property** (which can be continuing, or non-continuing), and
- a **power of attorney for personal care**.

---

1 SO 1992, c. 30.

Power of Attorney for Property

A power of attorney for property grants a person the legal authorization to act on someone's behalf and make binding decisions about his or her property and finances. Unless the grantor (in other words, the person who gives the power of attorney) states otherwise, the power granted to an attorney is quite broad and authorizes him or her "to do on the grantor's behalf anything in respect of property that the grantor could do if capable, except make a will."[2]

Scope of Attorney's Powers

The activities that the attorney for property is authorized to perform typically include banking, signing cheques and documents, purchasing items, and paying bills. They can also include managing investments, paying taxes, buying or selling real property, and initiating or defending a lawsuit. The grantor, can, however, limit the powers given to the attorney. For example, the grantor may state that the attorney can sign the grantor's banking documents only while the grantor is out of the country and/or only for a specified period of time.

Creating a Power of Attorney for Property

Anyone who is at least 18 years old and "mentally capable" can give a valid power of attorney for property. Mental capacity means that the person giving the power of attorney knows or understands the following:

- the kind and approximate value of his or her property;
- his or her obligations to **dependants**;
- the nature and extent of what the attorney is authorized to do on his/her behalf;
- that the attorney is accountable for all decisions he/she makes about the person's property;
- that he/she may **revoke** the continuing power of attorney (if capable);
- that the value of his/her property may decrease if the attorney does not manage it wisely; and
- that there is a risk of the attorney misusing his/her authority.

dependants
people who depend on another person for financial support

revoke
cancel or nullify

The decision whether or not to appoint a power of attorney for property is a personal one; there is no legal requirement to have a power of attorney for property. If a person becomes mentally incapable (discussed below) and does not have a power of attorney, a friend or relative can apply to be appointed to act on that person's behalf. As a last resort, the Office of the Public Guardian and Trustee (OPGT) can apply to be appointed to act on a person's behalf when no one else is available. If this happens, the OPGT is called the person's "guardian of property."

---

2 Ibid., s. 7(2).

Appointing an Attorney

The person who is appointed to make decisions on behalf of the grantor is called an "attorney for property." He or she must be at least 18 years old.

As noted above, a person can appoint more than one attorney. In this case, unless the power of attorney states otherwise, the attorneys must act jointly. In other words, they must agree on all decisions. If, on the other hand, the power of attorney states that the attorneys may act independently and make decisions separately, then they are acting jointly and severally. For example, assume Jumeel has a power of attorney for property which names both Spiro and Althea as attorneys. If the power of attorney authorizes Spiro and Althea to act jointly and severally, then either Spiro or Althea can act alone and make a decision independently about Jumeel's property. If, however, the power of attorney is silent on this point, or specifically requires that Spiro and Althea make all property decisions jointly, then neither one of them can make a decision alone; they must act jointly.

Continuing Versus Non-Continuing Powers of Attorney

A power of attorney for property can be either a continuing power of attorney or a non-continuing power of attorney (also known as a general power of attorney). A power of attorney is continuing if it is called a continuing power of attorney for property, or if it authorizes the attorney to continue to act on the grantor's behalf and make binding decisions about property even if the grantor becomes mentally incapable. A continuing power of attorney, which survives incapacity, is much more common than a non-continuing power of attorney.

A non-continuing, or general, power of attorney means that the attorney can act on the grantor's behalf only while the grantor is mentally capable. In other words, if the grantor becomes incapable of managing his or her property, the non-continuing power of attorney automatically ends. This type of power of attorney is typically only used to authorize someone to act for a specific reason and/or for a limited period of time—for example, when the grantor will be out of the country for an extended period of time.

For the rest of this chapter, any reference to "power of attorney for property" refers to a continuing power of attorney for property.

Execution

A power of attorney for property must be signed in the presence of two witnesses, each of whom must also sign the document. The *Substitute Decisions Act* disqualifies the following people from acting as a witness:

- the spouse or partner of either the grantor or the attorney;
- the grantor's child, or someone the grantor treats as his/her child;
- someone who has a guardian of property; or
- someone under the age of 18.

It should be noted that the terms "spouse" and "partner" are given a very broad meaning under the statute. For example, a *partner* is defined as "either of two persons who have lived together for at least one year and have a close personal relationship that is of primary importance in both persons' lives."[3] A *spouse* is defined as a person

    (a) to whom the person is married, or
    (b) with whom the person is living in a conjugal relationship outside marriage,
if the two persons,
        (i) have cohabited for at least one year,
        (ii) are together the parents of a child, or
        (iii) have together entered into a cohabitation agreement under section 53
of the *Family Law Act*.[4]

Effective Date

A power of attorney for property becomes effective as soon as it is properly signed and witnessed, unless it states otherwise. The usual wording in a power of attorney is as follows: "This power of attorney comes into effect on the date it is signed and witnessed." This means that the attorney is legally entitled to start using the power right away. In other words, while the grantor is still capable, both the grantor and the attorney can sign documents and make decisions on the grantor's behalf.

For example, assume Serena creates a power of attorney for property and names Sharif as the attorney. While Serena is capable, she can choose to make her own decisions and take necessary actions with respect to her property and finances. However, she can also ask Sharif to do these things on her behalf, in the event Serena is unavailable when decisions must be made or actions must be taken regarding her property.

When creating a power of attorney for property, a grantor may include a provision stating that the attorney cannot act unless and until the grantor becomes mentally incapable. Where such a provision is included, the grantor, so long as he or she is mentally capable, is the only person who can make decisions about his or her finances and property, notwithstanding the fact that a continuing power of attorney for property has been created.

Mental Incapacity

Pursuant to the *Substitute Decisions Act*, a person is incapable of managing property if he or she is unable to understand essential information necessary to make a particular property-related decision or to appreciate the implications of making a specific decision or of making no decision.

As mentioned above, if a person becomes incapable of managing property, his or her attorney can act on his or her behalf and make property-related decisions only

---

3 Ibid., s. 1(1).

4 Ibid.

if the power of attorney is a continuing one. If it is a general or non-continuing power of attorney for property, the attorney's powers are automatically terminated once the grantor becomes incapable of doing so him- or herself.

A person may give a general power of attorney to one person and a continuing power of attorney to another. For example, assume that Benny is selling his house and wants to authorize his lawyer to sign documents related to the sale of the house but to do nothing else. Assume also that Benny wants his brother Kenny to be his attorney for property, with unlimited powers. Benny should create two powers of attorney for property:

1. a general or non-continuing power of attorney for property which appoints his lawyer as his attorney and limits his lawyer's power to signing only those documents that are required to complete the sale of his house; and

2. a continuing power of attorney for property which appoints Kenny as his attorney.

As this example illustrates, a general or non-continuing power of attorney for property can be used together with a continuing power of attorney for property.

Revocation and Termination

A power of attorney for property remains valid and effective until it is either terminated or revoked. The grantor can revoke the power of attorney at any time, provided he or she is still capable of managing property. For example, assume Jumeel wants to revoke his power of attorney for property that names Spiro and Althea as attorneys. As long as Jumeel is competent and is able to make decisions about his property, he can revoke his power of attorney. Jumeel cannot revoke it, however, if he becomes mentally incapable.

revocation
cancellation of a
power of attorney

To revoke a power of attorney, the grantor must state that he or she is revoking it. This must be done in writing, in a document called a **revocation**. A revocation must be signed and witnessed in the same way that a continuing power of attorney for property must be, as discussed above.

As long as he is mentally capable, Jumeel can also give a new power of attorney. For example, assume that Jumeel has lost trust in Spiro and Althea. He now wants Jasmine to be his attorney. Instead of revoking his existing power of attorney for property, he can create a new one, naming Jasmine as his attorney and stating that it revokes the former one. However, it is safer for Jumeel to actually revoke the former power of attorney. This would provide clarity and would prevent any misuse by Spiro and Althea. It should also be noted that when signing on behalf of a grantor, the attorney must present the original power of attorney document as authority for his/her ability to act on the grantor's behalf. In this situation, therefore, Jumeel does not actually have to revoke the power of attorney if he has the original document in his possession. He can simply tear it up to make sure that Spiro and Althea cannot use it.

It is possible to have multiple powers of attorney. For example, if Jumeel wants Jasmine to be his attorney in addition to Spiro and Althea, he can create a new power of attorney that appoints Jasmine as his attorney for property. This second attorney for property does not revoke the earlier one. The two powers of attorney can coexist, and each is legally effective. This means that Spiro and Althea have the authority to act jointly on behalf of Jumeel, and Jasmine has the authority to act independently on behalf of Jumeel. This can prove useful if, for example, Spiro and Althea take a last-minute trip and are therefore unavailable to act on Jumeel's behalf. By creating a second power of attorney appointing Jasmine, Jumeel can feel assured that someone will be available to make decisions and act on his behalf, if necessary. A continuing power of attorney for property terminates when the grantor dies, or when

- the attorney dies, resigns, or becomes incapable of managing property (this termination does not occur if there is a co-attorney, or a substitute attorney who is willing and able to act);
- the court appoints a guardian of property for the grantor;
- the grantor signs a new continuing power of attorney, unless the grantor states that he/she wants to have multiple continuing powers of attorney; or
- the grantor revokes it.

Power of Attorney for Personal Care

Scope of Attorney's Powers

This type of power of attorney is similar to a power of attorney for property in the following respect: it appoints someone to make decisions on the grantor's behalf, but is effective only if the grantor becomes mentally incapable. The types of decisions that can be made by an attorney for personal care are very different, however, from those that can be made by an attorney for property. An attorney for personal care cannot make decisions about property or finances; he or she can make personal care decisions only. Personal care decisions include decisions about medical treatment, health care, housing, clothing, nutrition, hygiene, and safety.

Creating a Power of Attorney for Personal Care

Anyone who is at least 16 years old is capable of giving a power of attorney for personal care provided he or she understands

- whether the proposed attorney is genuinely concerned about his/her health and safety; and
- that the proposed attorney may need to make decisions for him/her.

As long as the grantor is able to understand these two things when he or she executes the power of attorney for personal care, the power of attorney is valid, even if the grantor is incapable of making personal care decisions at that time. "Incapable of making personal care decisions" means that "the person is not able to understand information that is relevant to making a decision concerning his or her own health care, nutrition, shelter, clothing, hygiene or safety, or is not able to appreciate the reasonably foreseeable consequences of a decision or lack of decision."[5]

As with a power of attorney for property, the decision about whether to appoint a power of attorney for personal care is a personal decision; there is no legal requirement to appoint one. If a person becomes mentally incapable (discussed below) and does not have a power of attorney for personal care, a family member has the right to make decisions about medical care or about admission to a long-term care facility on that person's behalf. As a last resort, if there is no one who is available to act on behalf of a mentally incapable person, the Office of the Public Guardian and Trustee will act as the attorney.

Appointing an Attorney

The person named in the power of attorney for personal care is called an "attorney for personal care." He or she must be at least 16 years old and can be, but does not have to be, the same person as the grantor's attorney for property. In fact, because personal care decisions differ so greatly from property or finance-related decisions, many people will name one person as their attorney for property and a different person as their attorney for personal care. For example, assume Carolina is creating a power of attorney for personal care. If Carolina's brother is an accountant and her best friend is a physician, Carolina will likely name her brother as her attorney for property and her best friend as her attorney for personal care.

As with a continuing power of attorney for property, the grantor can appoint more than one attorney. Co-attorneys for personal care must act jointly, unless the power of attorney states that they can act jointly and severally.

A person cannot act as an attorney for personal care if he or she is being paid to provide the grantor with health care or with training, support, residential, or social services. For example, a caregiver cannot be an attorney for personal care unless that caregiver is the grantor's spouse, partner, or relative. As with powers of attorney for property, the terms "spouse" and "partner" are broadly defined in the legislation (see above).

Execution

A power of attorney for personal care must be signed in the presence of two witnesses, each of whom must also sign the document. The persons who are disqualified from being witnesses to a power of attorney for property are also disqualified from being witnesses to a power of attorney for personal care. (See the discussion above of execution and disqualification under the *Substitute Decisions Act*.)

---

5   Ibid., s. 45.

Effective Date

Unlike a power of attorney for property, which (unless it states otherwise) takes effect as soon as it is executed, a power of attorney for personal care takes effect only if the grantor is mentally incapable of making his or her own personal care decisions. In other words, the powers granted to an attorney for personal care are effective only if and when the grantor becomes incapable; they cannot be used, and no personal care decisions can be made on the grantor's behalf, before this point of incapacity is reached. If the grantor is capable of making some personal care decisions but not others, then the attorney for personal care can only make the personal care decisions that the grantor is not capable of making.

Mental Incapacity

As mentioned above, a power of attorney for personal care is not effective unless the grantor becomes mentally incapable—in other words, unable to understand essential information necessary to make a particular personal care decision or to appreciate the implications of making a specific decision or of making no decision.

The *Substitute Decisions Act* provides the following:

> A person is incapable of personal care if the person is not able to understand information that is relevant to making a decision concerning his or her own health care, nutrition, shelter, clothing, hygiene or safety, or is not able to appreciate the reasonably foreseeable consequences of a decision or lack of decision.[6]

In most cases, a doctor determines whether the grantor has become mentally incapable. If the personal care decision is not about medical treatment or admission to a long-term facility, then either the attorney or the grantor's doctor can determine whether the grantor has become mentally incapable. Once incapacity is established, the attorney for personal care can start making medical decisions on the grantor's behalf. However, if the grantor gave someone else (in his/her power of attorney for personal care) the power to confirm mental incapacity, then the attorney cannot make personal care decisions until that person confirms the grantor's incapacity.

For example, assume JoLinda has a power of attorney for personal care that names Tony as her attorney but states that her family doctor, Dr. Carson, must confirm her mental incapacity. Tony may think JoLinda has become incapable, but he cannot start making personal care decisions for JoLinda until Dr. Carson assesses her and confirms that she is in fact mentally incapable of making those decisions herself.

For personal care decisions about medical treatment or admission to a long-term care facility, the decision about mental incapacity can be made only by a health professional, regardless of who the grantor names in his or her power of attorney for personal care. Assume, for example, that a health professional is proposing medical treatment or admission to a long-term care facility for a person who has an attorney

---

6   Ibid., s. 45.

for personal care who has been authorized to make such a decision. Under the *Health Care Consent Act, 1996*,[7] only the health professional can decide whether that person is mentally incapable. If the health professional determines that the person is not capable of making a decision for him/herself, then the person's attorney for personal care can make the decision about medical treatment or a long-term care facility.

It should be noted that if the grantor is still capable of making some personal care decisions, but not others, his or her attorney can make only the decisions the grantor is incapable of making him- or herself.

Revocation and Termination

A power of attorney for personal care is revoked in the same way that a power of attorney for property is revoked, as discussed above. A person is considered capable of revoking his/her power of attorney for personal care if he or she has the required mental capacity to create one (see above, under the heading "Creating a Power of Attorney for Personal Care").

A continuing power of attorney for personal care terminates when the grantor dies, or when

- the attorney dies, resigns, or becomes incapacitated, unless there is a co-attorney, or a substitute attorney who is willing and able to act;
- the court appoints a guardian for the grantor;
- the grantor signs a new power of attorney for personal care, unless the grantor states that he/she wants to have multiple powers of attorney for personal care; or
- the grantor revokes it.

Living Will Clause

A power of attorney for personal care may contain a living will clause. This is an important provision because it confirms the grantor's wish that no heroic measures should be taken in order to sustain the grantor's life if there is no reasonable chance of him/her recovering from a serious illness or disability. For example, a grantor may not want to be kept alive on artificial life support if he or she becomes seriously ill and there is no realistic expectation of his or her recovering. The grantor can include a living will clause in the power of attorney for personal care, directing his/her attorney to withdraw life support in these circumstances. This saves the attorney from having to make the very difficult decision concerning whether to withdraw life support.

---

7 SO 1996, c. 2, Sched. A.

KEY TERMS

attorney, 132
dependants, 133
incapacity, 132
jointly, 132
jointly and severally, 132

power of attorney, 132
power of attorney for personal care, 132
power of attorney for property, 132
revocation, 136
revoke, 133

REVIEW QUESTIONS

1. How does a power of attorney differ from a will?

2. What is the difference between a power of attorney for property and a power of attorney for personal care?

3. Gerardo wants to appoint both his son and daughter as his attorneys for property and prefers that they make all decisions together. When preparing his power of attorney, what should Gerardo do to ensure that his children always act together? Explain your answer.

4. Lucia is 15 years old. Can she give a power of attorney? Explain your answer.

5. Phillipe is preparing a power of attorney for property and is appointing Juan as his attorney. Juan is not married but lives with his girlfriend Suzette. Can Suzette act as a witness when Phillipe signs the power of attorney?

6. Jose signed a power of attorney for property last December, appointing Georgina as his attorney. There are no limitations on the power granted to Georgina. Jose is mentally competent but would like Georgina to sign some documents on his behalf. Can Georgina do this? Explain your answer.

7. Rose would like to revoke her power of attorney for property, which names Tran as her attorney. Can Rose do this? Explain your answer.

8. Rashid is 17 years old and wants to give two powers of attorney—one for property and the other for personal care—each naming his aunt Lashana as his attorney. Explain whether or not Rashid is capable of giving these two powers of attorney.

9. Devan is adamant that he never wants to be kept artificially alive by a machine in the event of an illness or an accident. What is the best way for Devan to convey his wishes?

10. Bruce is going to Florida for the winter and is in the process of selling his house. He wants to allow his daughter Janeel to sign the sale documents for the house if it sells while he is away. What type of document should Bruce sign before he leaves?

Glossary

A

abatement the reduction of a gift when there is not enough money in the estate to pay the entire gift

abstract book a book in the Registry System that records registered interests in land

ademption the failing of a gift that no longer exists

administration bond of indemnity money that is secured with a third party and paid out in the event that the estate trustee does not pay a person entitled to be paid from the estate

adverse interest in land an interest in someone else's land that is acquired by using that person's land, without permission, for a certain period of time

adverse possession valid title to land acquired through open, visible, and uninterrupted possession of that property, without the owner's permission, for a period of at least 10 years

adversely without the owner's permission

affidavit of execution a document that is signed by one of the witnesses to a will and that swears to the fact that both witnesses were present when the will was signed

agreement of purchase and sale a contract between a buyer (purchaser) and seller (vendor) of real property

amortization period the length of time it takes to repay a loan in full if the schedule of monthly payments in the charge is followed

articles of amalgamation the document that must be registered when two corporations amalgamate (join)

articles of dissolution the document that must be registered when a corporation voluntarily dissolves (closes down)

articles of incorporation the legal document that sets out a corporation's purpose and that, when filed, creates the corporation

assuming a mortgage taking over an existing mortgage

attorney the person who is named or appointed to act on behalf of someone else (in a power of attorney)

auditor a person appointed by a corporation to oversee its financial matters

automated title index a computerized printout listing all documents registered on title

B

balance due date the date that the term of a mortgage ends

balloon payment the final payment for the amount of principal that remains unpaid at the end of the term of a charge

beneficiary an entity that receives a gift under a will

blended payment a charge payment combining principal and interest into regular equal monthly payments

board of directors all of the directors of a corporation

business style name/trade name the registered name—not the actual name of the corporation—that a company uses to conduct its business

buy–sell agreement an agreement between partners that defines how one partner can buy out the interest of the other partner(s) (also known as a buyout agreement)

bylaws rules that govern the operation of a corporation

143

bylaws (municipal) laws that are passed by a municipality

C

capital the financial investment contributed to a business

Certificate of Appointment of Estate Trustee With a Will the document that is provided by the court to prove the authority of the estate trustee named in the will

Certificate of Appointment of Estate Trustee Without a Will the document the court provides to prove the authority of a person applying to be an estate trustee without a will

chattels movable possessions not attached to real property

closed mortgage a mortgage that prohibits repayment of the loan (unless a penalty is paid) before the expiry of the term

codicil a legal document that amends a will

commit waste destroy, abuse, or make permanent undesirable changes to real property

common shares a class of shares that typically include the right to vote

conflict of interest occurs when a person in a position of trust has a conflict between his/her personal interests and his/her professional interests

copyright the exclusive "right to copy" a writer's, artist's, or musician's original work

corporate seal a device, used to emboss paper, that confirms the authority of an individual to sign on behalf of the corporation

covenant a personal promise to pay

creditor a party to whom money is owed

D

deed a document that transfers ownership of land

degree of consanguinity the closeness of legal relationships within a family

demonstrative legacy an amount of money to be paid from the estate from a particular source

dependants people who depend on another person for financial support

derivative action a remedy, available to shareholders, that permits a shareholder to bring an action in the name of the corporation

devise a gift of real property

discharge of charge/mortgage a document registered on title when a charge is paid off; given by the chargee to the chargor confirming that the loan has been paid in full and extinguishing the chargee's interest in the property

dividend a payment made to shareholders, which represents a portion of a corporation's profits

doctrine of escheat a common-law doctrine providing that if a landowner dies without a will and without heirs to inherit his or her land, the land will revert to the Crown

dominant tenement land that benefits from an easement

E

easement the right to use a portion of someone else's land for a specific purpose, without requiring the owner's permission each time the land is used

easement by prescription an easement right to someone else's land that is acquired after a period of open and uninterrupted use

encroachment a building or structure intruding upon someone else's land

encroachment agreement an agreement between neighbours that deals with an encroachment issue and clears up title

encroachment by prescription the right to keep an encroaching building or structure on land after it has remained there for 20 years

encumbrancer a party who has a charge, claim, or lien registered against someone's real property

encumbrances charges, claims, liens, or liabilities that affect title to a property

equalization of net family property a monetary adjustment made between legally married spouses (upon separation, divorce, or death) to balance or equalize their respective net family property values

equity the net value of property after the value of the encumbrances is deducted

escheats the reversion of property to the Crown

estate (property law) an interest in land that provides the right to exclusive possession

estate (wills and estates) the total of everything a person owned immediately before he or she died

estate administration tax the tax that is paid when an estate is probated

estate trustee a person who is appointed to carry out the instructions of a deceased person

exclusive possession sole possession of the land; denial of possession to all others

executed signed by the testator and witnessed by two people who are present at the same time as the testator

execution the short name for a writ of execution

express grant creation of an easement by written document from the owner of the servient tenement to the owner of the dominant tenement

expropriate reacquire land while compensating the owners; something the Crown is entitled to do for public purposes

extinguished brought to an end

extra-provincial licence a licence that authorizes a corporation to conduct its business in another province

F

fair dealing exemptions uses of someone else's copyright that are not considered an infringement of copyright

fair market value the amount that property would sell for in the open market

fee simple estate the right to exclusive possession and the right to dispose of the land for an indefinite period of time; most absolute form of ownership

fiduciary duty the duty to act honestly, in good faith, and in the best interests of someone or something (such as a corporation)

financial statement a written report, usually prepared by an accountant, that provides details about the financial aspects of the corporation

first dealing the first transaction after property is converted from the Registry System to the Land Titles System

first director the individual(s) appointed by the incorporator to act as a director until the first shareholders' meeting

fixed interest rate a rate of interest that remains the same for the term of the charge

fixtures chattels that have become attached or affixed to real property; immovable possessions attached to real property

foreclosure a court action whereby the chargee obtains legal title to the property after default by the chargor

forfeit lose the right

fundamental change a change that will affect the corporation and that requires two-thirds of all shareholder votes

G

general legacy an amount of money to be paid from the estate without mentioning a particular source

goodwill the intangible component of the value of a business, such as the business's reputation

grant a document that transfers ownership of land

guardian a person named in a will to take care of minor children

H

holograph will a will that is entirely handwritten and signed by the testator (and not witnessed)

I

identification theory of corporate liability the theory used to describe the liability of a corporation when the person who commits a tort or crime is the "directing mind" of the corporation

incapacity inability to understand essential information necessary to make a particular personal care or property-related decision or to appreciate the implications of making a specific decision or of making no decision

incorporate the process of creating a corporation

incorporator the person who signs and files the articles of incorporation

industrial design the aesthetic aspects of a finished product; its visual appeal, not its function

infringement of copyright occurs when someone (other than the copyright owner) does something that only the copyright owner can do, without the owner's permission

injunction a court order requiring a party to refrain from doing a specific act

insider trading when the director of a corporation has access to non-public material information about an investment and uses this inside information to his or her advantage

insolvent an entity that is unable to meet its financial obligations as they become due

institutional lender a bank, trust company, credit union, or insurance company that is in the business of lending money

intellectual property a creation or invention of the mind

interest the amount, added to the principal amount of a loan, that the mortgagor must pay in return for the right to obtain and use the money advanced

interest adjustment date (IAD) the date on which an adjustment is made for interest that accumulates between the date the loan was advanced and the charge payment date for the following month; assuming charge payments are made monthly, this date will be one month before the date of the first regular payment

interest rate the percentage of interest, on an annual basis, that the mortgagee charges the mortgagor on the principal amount of money borrowed under a loan

interests in land rights to use someone else's land that are not estates and do not confer a right to exclusive possession of the land

intestate not having a will upon death

inventor's claims the claims included in the specification; defines the boundaries of an inventor's patent protection

J

joint and several liability state in which (1) each partner is fully liable for the full amount of a creditor's claim or debt, and (2) the partner who pays the full amount can claim against the other partner(s) for the other's share of the claim or debt

joint liability each partner is fully liable for the full amount of the partnership's debts or of claims against the partnership

joint tenants two or more people in an ownership arrangement whereby, on the death of one owner, the survivor(s) inherits the deceased's share

jointly together; the term applied to an arrangement whereby multiple attorneys cannot act independently

jointly and severally the term applied to an arrangement whereby multiple attorneys can make decisions separately, independent of each other

judicial sale the sale of charged property ordered and administered by a court

judicial the authority of a court

L

Land Titles System a land registration system in Ontario governed by the *Land Titles Act*

lapse what happens to a gift when the beneficiary predeceases the testator

leasehold estate the right to exclusive possession of the property for a specified period of time in return for the payment of rent

leave permission of the court

legal description a description of land that is used in documents creating an interest in land; describes the land with reference to recorded maps, surveys, or plans

legal entity an individual or business that is responsible for its actions and has the right to enter into contracts, assume and enforce obligations, and sue or be sued

letters patent another term for patent

life estate a person's right to exclusive possession of the property for the length of his or her life

life tenant the owner of a life estate

limited liability liability that is limited by law or by agreement; in the case of a corporation, it refers to the lack of personal liability, on the part of shareholders, directors, and officers, for the acts of the corporation

liquidated converted into cash or equivalents through sale

M

metes and bounds description a written description of the boundaries and dimensions of a parcel of land

minute book the book containing all of the documents of the corporation

minutes the written record of a shareholders' or directors' meeting

mortgage/charge a loan that is secured by real property

mortgagee a lender who uses real property as security for a loan

mortgagee/chargee the lender in a mortgage transaction

mortgagor/chargor the borrower in a mortgage transaction

N

net family property the net value (value of total assets at date of separation, divorce, or death less value of assets at date of marriage) of a person's assets

non-blended payment a charge payment that does not blend or combine principal and interest into equal payments; the amount of principal (if any) repaid each month is a fixed amount and the calculation of interest is based on the outstanding principal at the time

not-for-profit corporation a corporation that is created for purposes—for example, charitable, educational, or religious purposes—other than making money for the benefit of the shareholders

notice of sale under mortgage a form served when the mortgagee commences power-of-sale proceedings

NUANS (Newly Upgraded Automated Name Search) a computerized search that is conducted to find existing business names and trademarks

numbered company a company that uses as its name the number assigned to it at the time of incorporation

O

officer an individual who manages the day-to-day functioning of a corporation

open mortgage a mortgage that permits repayment of the loan before the expiry of the term

oppression remedy a remedy, available to shareholders, that permits a shareholder to apply to the court for relief if the shareholder feels that the actions of the corporation—or any use of the directors' powers—have been oppressive or unfairly prejudicial

ordinary resolution a decision made by a majority (at least 51 percent) of all shareholder votes

P

parcel register the book in the Land Titles System that records all registered interests in land

partially open mortgage a closed mortgage with some repayment provisions

partnership agreement an agreement between partners that defines the terms of their relationship

passing of accounts the formal process required in order to justify the estate trustee's compensation

patent infringement interference with the patent holder's exclusive rights to produce, use, sell, or otherwise take advantage of his/her patented invention, without permission

patent an exclusive right (granted by the government upon application by an inventor) to produce, use, sell, or otherwise take advantage of an invention for a period of 20 years

per stirpes a method of distributing a gift to children pursuant to a will, which provides that if the child predeceases the testator, the child's share is divided equally among his or her children (the testator's grandchildren)

personal liability a business owner's personal responsibility for the debts and obligations of the business

personal property chattels; property that is not real property

petition a formal request to the Commissioner of Patents to grant a patent

piercing the corporate veil (or lifting the corporate veil) process whereby a court, under certain circumstances—for example, where the corporation has engaged in fraud or other wrongful acts—disregards the corporation's legally separate existence and makes the directors, officers, and/or shareholders personally responsible for the corporation's actions

plaintiff the party that initiates a lawsuit

power of attorney a document that provides legal authorization to act on behalf of someone else and to make binding decisions for him/her

power of attorney for personal care provides legal authorization to act on someone's behalf and make binding personal care decisions for him or her

power of attorney for property provides legal authorization to act on someone's behalf and make binding decisions for him or her about property and finances

power of sale the power to exercise the remedy of sale in case of default under a charge (for example, the mortgagee can sell the property to a third party when the mortgagor is in default)

preferential share the first $200,000 of an estate that goes to the deceased's spouse when a person dies intestate

preferred shares a class of shares that typically give their owners the right to be paid out before the owners of common shares are paid out

prepayment penalty an amount that a borrower may have to pay when ending a mortgage contract earlier than the balance due date

prescription the means by which an interest is acquired in someone else's land after a period of open and uninterrupted use

prime lending rate the interest rate charged by banks to their largest, most secure, and most creditworthy customers on short-term loans

principal the amount of money borrowed

priority the interest of a mortgagee that is in preference to another mortgagee

private corporation a small corporation with few shareholders that does not offer its shares to the public

private lender an individual or business that lends money but is not a bank, trust company, credit union, or insurance company

probate fees an estate administration tax; the estate trustee must pay this tax when applying for a Certificate of Appointment of Estate Trustee (with or without a will)

probate/probated the court process by which a will is proved valid or invalid and which now involves the estate trustee's obtaining either a Certificate of Appointment of Estate Trustee With a Will or a Certificate of Appointment of Estate Trustee Without a Will

property identifier number (PIN) a unique nine-digit number for each property; used to gain access to the automated title index

proxy the document that permits a shareholder to vote by mail or to appoint someone else to attend the meeting and vote on the shareholder's behalf

public corporation a corporation with many shareholders that offers its shares, which are traded on the stock market, to the general public

Q

quorum the minimum number of people required to make a decision

R

real property land, including everything that is attached to it

redemption period the 35-day period, after the chargor is in default, during which the chargor has the opportunity to put the charge back into good standing and redeem the property, and the chargee cannot take any steps to redeem the property

reference plan a registered plan that illustrates the boundaries of a parcel of land

refinance obtain a mortgage on property currently owned

registered head office the address of the corporation

registered patent agent a person who has training in patent law and specializes in patent applications

registered plan of subdivision a plan that is registered on title illustrating the measurements and boundaries of all lots and streets created by the division of a large parcel of land into many smaller lots

Registry System a land registration system in Ontario governed by the *Registry Act*

remainderman the term used to refer to the owner in fee simple who must wait until a life estate ends before acquiring possession of a property

residue what is left of a testator's assets after the specific bequests have been distributed

residue of the estate everything that is left over after debts have been paid and specific gifts have been distributed

resolution a decision made by a corporation's directors or shareholders

restrictive covenant a promise by an owner of land to refrain from doing something on the property

revocation cancellation of a power of attorney

revoke cancel or nullify

right of survivorship automatic vesting of an interest in the surviving joint tenant or tenants when one joint tenant dies

right of way the right to use a portion of another's land for access purposes

root deed (root of title) the first conveyance of the fee simple estate (a deed, grant, or transfer) registered before the commencement date of a title search

S

search the title conduct an investigation into the status and history of title to land

security what the lender/chargee/mortgagee receives in exchange for lending money

servient tenement land over which an easement runs

set-back requirement a provision in a bylaw stating the minimum required distance between structures and a lot line

sham something that is not what it purports to be (that is, false, not genuine)

share a unit of ownership in a corporation

share certificate a written document that states the number of shares owned by a shareholder

shareholder a corporation or an individual that owns shares in a company

shelf corporation/shelf company a company that does not carry on any business and is created for the sole purpose of being available to someone who needs to start a company quickly

silent partner someone who contributes money or property to a firm but takes no part in its management or day-to-day business

sole proprietor the owner of a sole proprietorship

sole proprietorship a business that is owned and operated by one person

special resolution a decision made by two-thirds of all shareholder votes

specific bequest a gift of named property (including an amount of money) to a beneficiary in a will

specific legacy a gift of a specific item

specification a detailed description of the invention contained in an application for a patent

standard charge terms mortgage terms setting out the obligations of the mortgagor and the rights of the mortgagee; used in all mortgages issued by an institutional lender

stock market a market where shares are publicly traded

surplus an amount left over after paying the mortgage, following a sale under power of sale

survivorship application the document that gets registered on title to prove the right of survivorship in a joint tenancy

T

tenants-in-common two or more people in an ownership arrangement whereby, on the death of one owner, the deceased's share passes to his or her heirs rather than to the other owners; no right of survivorship

term the length of time that the borrower and lender are bound by the mortgage contract

testamentary intent the intent to dispose of assets in a will

testator a person who dies with a valid will

title the legal right to the ownership and possession of property; evidence of such a right

title opinion a lawyer's statement as to whether or not title to a property is good

trade name the name that a sole proprietorship, partnership, or corporation uses to carry on business

trademark a word(s), design, slogan, symbol, logo, or any other mark (or a combination of these) that identifies and distinguishes a person's goods or services from those of all others

U

unanimous resolution a decision about the corporation that requires 100 percent of all shareholder votes

undue influence when someone in a position of power exerts pressure on another person to sign a document, even though it may not be in that person's best interest

unincorporated business a business that has not been incorporated

V

variable interest rate a rate of interest that fluctuates with changing market conditions during the term of the charge

vendor take-back mortgage a charge created when the seller agrees to lend the buyer money toward the purchase price of the property, and the buyer gives the seller a charge on the property as security for the loan

vests provides an immediate right to present or future ownership or possession

W

will/last will and testament a written document that dictates what happens to a person's estate when the person dies

writ of execution a judicial order addressed to the sheriff requiring the enforcement of a judgment

written resolutions decisions that the corporation's directors or shareholders make in writing instead of at a formal meeting

Index